sacred circles

For my dear friend, Diane
In remembrance of
that magical evening
with goddess images on the
beach ...!
          Love always,
               Ellen

     Spring, 1998

sacred Circles

A Guide to Creating Your Own Women's Spirituality Group

Robin Deen Carnes and Sally Craig

HarperSanFrancisco
A Division of HarperCollinsPublishers

HarperCollins Web Site: http://www.harpercollins.com
HarperCollins®, ♦®, and HarperSanFrancisco™ are trademarks of
HarperCollins Publishers Inc.

Book design by Martha Blegen

FIRST EDITION

Library of Congress Cataloging-in-Publication Data
Carnes, Robin
Sacred circles : a guide to creating your own women's spirituality group /
Robin Deen Carnes and Sally Craig. — 1st ed.
        p.   cm.
Includes bibliographical references and index.
ISBN 0–06–251522–5 (pbk.)
1. Women—Religious life. 2. Women and religion. 3. Spiritual life.
4. Small groups—Religious aspects. I. Craig, Sally. II. Title.
BL625.7.C36 1998
291.4'082—dc21   97–13381

98 99 00 01 02 ❖ RRDH 10 9 8 7 6 5 4 3 2 1

For Peter Craig, my life-partner, safe haven, and heart's anchor.
For Katie, my beloved woman-child. Your spirit
truly brightens my days.

For Joshua, my most ecstatic creation. For always
giving me reasons to laugh and live.
And to Peter Carnes, my true love, at last.

Contents

Acknowledgments

We can't help but believe that this book wanted to be written. Every place we turned for help, we found it. Resources appeared, books fell off shelves. This is not to say that the book magically wrote itself. Hardly. But we felt guided and supported and protected at every turn.

We must have had a secret coconspirator and coauthor out there, and we choose to call her Spirit. Thank you, Spirit, for your endless and juicy generosity.

On a more mundane but no less important level, many people have helped us along the way, and we want to acknowledge a few of them here. At the inception of this project, we invited a group of wise women to serve as our midwives, a virtual circle of support. Some of them read chapters and gave us helpful feedback, some of them advised us on specific questions, and all of them held us in their hearts. To each of them we give thanks:

Gertrude Banks, Sally's grandmother, who died before the book was finished;

Dorothy Mae Taylor, Robin's feisty, funny, huge-hearted grandmother;

Caroline Banks and Bettie Deen, our mothers and kindred spirits;

Ria Portocarrero, love warrior extraordinaire;

Colleen Kelley, visionary artist and desert ceremonialist;

Sarah Fahy and Cita Lamb, rekindlers of ancient memories;

Joanna Macy, Sally's spiritual sister and role model;

Jean Bartunek, Robin's wise friend and grad school professor; and

Ruthmarijke Smeding, Dutch goddess and all-around great woman.

I, Sally, have a large, extended family, at the heart of which is my husband, Peter, our grown daughter, Katie, and her new husband, Piers. You are each nurturers and anchors for me, sources of steadfast love and support. Ellen Barlow lives with us and radiates a powerful life force. Jenny Craig radiates hers from long distance. Among my friends, I would especially like to thank Elizabeth Fox and Ruth Caplan for their daily and enthusiastic interest in this project. Sunny Pietrafesa provides the unconditional love that we all need. Bill and Caroline Banks, my parents, have spent the last twenty-eight years as independent booksellers on Cape Cod. Not only did they impart a love for reading, but they are my role models for living a life they love.

I, Robin, would like to let a few other people know how important they are to me and to thank them for supporting me through this book journey. Peter, for your gentle yet probing questions, for your confidence in me, for your quiet, profound intuition, and for forever surprising me with your tender, wise, expansive heart, I thank you. Our love is my fuel. Josh Reid, I thank you for being the most incredible son/ person I could ever hope to have birthed, much less befriended. Mom and Dad, thanks for the colorful palette of genes and traits you have passed me and for the exuberant confidence and support you have given me on this project. Thanks to Suzanne Lagay, Lisa Zoppetti, and Sarah Harris for loving me. And thanks to Ria Portocarrero and Connie Miller for teaching me the tools that help me dance through life.

Of course, our own women's group was what inspired us to write this in the first place. Each one of you is a splendid and sparkling facet of womanhood. We love you all: Bettie Deen, Laura Delaney, Laura Dicurcio, Jeanne Feeney, Elizabeth Fox, Elizabeth Friberg, Antoinette Kranenburg, Clair Oaks, Allison Porter, Susan Shearouse, Lois Taylor-Holsey, Sandra Van Fossen, and Lisa Zoppetti.

In the course of writing this book, we spoke with hundreds of women. We are especially grateful to the women we interviewed concerning their own groups, which we profile in chapter 2, and to those who wrote their stories in chapter 6. Wabun Wind, Hemitra Crecraft, and Sue King all shared their spirit and wide experience so generously. Our interviews with them ended up as full-fledged spiritual transmissions.

We had a wonderful forum for sharing our ideas about women's spirituality groups at the Washington National Cathedral, where we helped to produce two massive events, "Sacred Circles" and "Passionate Living: The Embodied Spirituality of Hildegard of Bingen." Our thanks to Carole Crumley, Grace Ogden, and Erik Schwarz. They are skilled at walking out on the edge.

Loretta Barrett, our agent, took on this book despite the fact that we had no track record. Sally had a "chance" encounter with Loretta at a conference in November 1995, and Loretta took us under her wing even though our only previous published work was a book commissioned by a supermarket trade association on the cost of employee turnover! We are grateful for her willingness to take a risk on us. Her assistant, Karen Gerwin-Stoopack, has been a real trouper in shepherding two first-time authors through the book publishing process.

We were blessed to have a wonderful editor, Caroline Pincus, who did a masterful job of helping us to focus on what was really important. Her empathy, savvy, and humor are an unbeatable combination, and we hope we are fortunate enough to have the chance to work with her again. Sally Kim, her editorial assistant, was also responsive and helpful and was there when we needed her. And Priscilla Stuckey copyedited our manuscript with compassionate attention.

Thanks also to Laura Delaney, Laura Dicurcio, and Jim Ronan for volunteering their wonderful photographic services.

And finally, our gratitude to all the pioneering and courageous women who have kept alive the traditions of women's spirituality.

Our Sacred Circle.
Back row (from left): Allison Porter, Sandra Van Fossen, Laura Dicurcio,
Antoinette Kranenburg, Elizabeth Fox.
Front row (from left): Susan Shearouse, Lisa Zoppetti, Jeanne Feeney, Robin
Carnes, Sally Craig, Laura Delaney, Bettie Deen, Clair Oaks.
Not pictured: Lois Taylor-Holsey and Elizabeth Friberg.

The dramatic action that we need to create a way of life on Earth that really works will be taken not through personal, social, or political action, but through spiritual action.

BROOKE MEDICINE EAGLE,
Buffalo Woman Comes Singing

Introduction
Becoming Teachers
for Each Other

There is nothing so wise as a circle.

RAINER MARIA RILKE

There is undeniable power in the shape of the circle. It is one of the fundamental energy patterns in the natural world. Circles collect and focus energy. We sit facing one another, mirroring one another, no one higher or more prominent. Women facing inward. The roundness of our circle reflects the roundness in our bodies. There is no outward diversion, no distraction from the focus on one another and ourselves. Circles are soothing, comforting, and challenging.

Our initiative to start our circle five years ago grew out of many years of exploration in all kinds of groups—consciousness-raising, support, therapy, twelve-step. By late 1992, we had each established our own individual spiritual practices. We also each had friends with whom we shared some spiritual matters. Yet we still felt a longing within us, a longing for a more intentional community in which to grow spiritually. We discovered that we yearned for communion with other women and the real intimacy that can come from a long-lasting commitment. We wanted a group different from all the others we had been in. It would be a "circle." We would sit in a circle and work in a circle, sharing leadership and responsibility for the group.

We wanted to establish different ground rules than those that govern everyday social discourse; we wanted a chance to speak plainly, a place to be intimately known, a setting to create ritual, to sing, and to dance, a collective forum where we could ask for and receive Spirit's guidance. So we set out to create our circle. We had no idea then what a powerful influence in our lives it would become.

In January 1993 our group was born—fifteen women, mothers, daughters, friends, sisters, white, black, American, and foreign born. We came together with the intention of forming long-term relationships, of making a commitment to one another and to our individual spiritual development.

After about two years, the group was going strong, and we knew that we had started something very special. We had created a sanctuary for ourselves, a place where we could sink into a deeper level of self-acceptance and affirmation, a place where we could come and drop the roles and facades and masks we habitually wear. It also has been a safe place to explore issues like sexuality and power and grace, taking delight in one another all the while.

Gradually the group began to meet people's deep need for belonging. It was a place where we could let down our defenses and be ourselves. Sometimes people wore makeup, sometimes not, sometimes a silly hat or a silky scarf. The policy was "come as you are" in this moment. Imagine! Liberated from having to show up a particular way, we felt a growing freedom to rediscover and express ourselves. We began experimenting with ritual, lighting candles, chanting, sitting in silence together, listening, and speaking with increased consciousness. Magic transpired. We walked away from meetings moved and different from when we arrived.

Since then, there is no doubt that the group has profoundly affected each one of us. This circle has evoked more radiance and happiness than either of us could have imagined. And more change. People have left relationships and jobs, gotten married, had babies, lost loved ones, and suffered life-threatening illnesses. The perspectives and contributions of group members have had tangible influences on how, and sometimes whether, these major life changes occurred. We all have been fed by watching one another grow. And this is food like no other. Delight as sacrament!

Whenever we talked about our circle with other women, they perked right up. And so we started nosing around. We found that on any given night in this region (and in yours, too, we suspect), women's circles are meeting—in homes, in churches and synagogues, in backyards, in hot tubs, at community centers. They are sprouting up like mushrooms after a summer rain. And an astonishing variety of mushrooms at that, and not one of them is poisonous!

But what, you may be wondering, other than a circle, makes a women's spirituality group different from any other bunch of friends? Though they come in lots of shapes and sizes, from Internet chat rooms to quarterly solstice gatherings to weekly prayer meetings, women's circles have some things in common. The members share life stories. They support and challenge one another. They are microcommunities.

In their compelling and wise book, *The Feminine Face of God: The Unfolding of the Sacred in Women,* Sherry Anderson and Patricia Hopkins write about the unique experience that women's circles bring to women's spiritual development. They describe women's circles as "containers of emergence." We love this image. Like a nest with fledglings at once hesitantly and boldly poking their heads out and venturing forth, women's circles provide a safe place where each person can begin trying her wings. In this time of heavy work and home demands, financial pressures, media blasting, and violence, women need a place just to be and become. A place where there is nothing to prove. A place where things are quieter and where there is an opportunity to listen, to oneself and others, intently.

At their essence, women's circles are a tool for discovering how Spirit is meant to manifest in your unique life, that is, in the particular form within which you are to channel love and light into this world. Are you a teacher, a healer, a writer, a mother, an artist, a businesswoman, an activist, a civic leader? What is your contribution, your voice? The speaking, the listening, the ritual, the intimate relationships with women so alike and so different within the container of the circle combine to create an alchemical reaction that transforms and purifies, bringing you closer and closer to your true Self. In short, it helps you to, as Marion Woodman puts it, "find the river of your life" and supports you in "surrendering to its current."

There is a vitality, a life force, a quickening that is translated through you into action, and because there is only one you in all time, this expression is unique. . . . You have to keep open and aware directly to the urges that motivate you. Keep the channel open.

MARTHA GRAHAM
in a letter to Agnes de Mille

xix

As we immersed ourselves in the subject of women's circles, we started finding them everywhere. And it seemed like every woman wanted to tell us about her circle. Why, we wondered, hasn't this phenomenon come to light? Why do some women feel isolated in their efforts? Why don't these groups know one another or at least know of one another's existence? What if they all came together once or twice a year in a gentle convocation of kindred spirits?

We could see just how empowering and encouraging it would be if we all knew about one another's existence. So we began to think about writing a book on women's circles, a book that would bring into the light the vast invisible network that we are a part of. And, of course, we wanted to inspire more women to share in this powerful experience.

As we looked around in the libraries and bookstores, we fully expected to find that someone had beaten us to the punch. There were many books on the Goddess, on Wicca, on women's issues, and on feminist spirituality, but we couldn't find a single book specifically about the kind of women's spirituality group we were seeking to propagate and celebrate. And so we leaped into envisioning and then writing this book.

A powerful inspiration to us was, ironically, a church-sponsored gathering. In July 1996, the National Cathedral in Washington, D.C., sponsored its first ever "Celebration of Women's Spirituality." Twelve hundred women from all walks of life gathered to explore and express their spirituality in a female-centered environment. We were on the organizing team. The cathedral staff expected a modest turnout and were dumbfounded when the event filled to capacity and people had to be turned away due to lack of space. Following that success, the cathedral then hosted "Passionate Living: The Embodied Spirituality of Hildegard of Bingen" in January 1997. Another sold-out crowd of nearly a thousand people, 90 percent of whom were women, came to learn more about this fascinating medieval prophetess, artist, poet, playwright, composer, herbalist, healer, and spiritual leader whose story is just now emerging from obscurity. Women flocked to the workshops we led on creating spiritual community.

We seek to inform, to inspire, and to catalyze. We will tell you how we and other women have started our groups. We will give you the tools you need to create your own special circle, from simple advice on meeting guidelines to suggestions for self-generated ritual. We hope this book will be useful to all of you who are already in women's circles, those of you who are interested in starting or joining one, and even those who don't intend to join one but just want to sample the experience.

We are neither academics nor journalists, and this book is not intended to be exhaustive or scholarly. It is authoritative only in that it is grounded in the truth of our own experience. This is fitting, we think, for the essence of women's spirituality is all about finding, trusting, speaking, and acting upon the truth of one's experience. And this truth, we assert, is all we ultimately have.

This book is our heart offering to women as we all begin to marshal the strength and courage necessary to claim our spiritual authority. Welcome to the ever-widening circle.

You will be teachers for each other. You will come together in circles and speak your truth to each other. The time has come for women to accept their spiritual responsibility for the planet.

SHERRY RUTH ANDERSON
AND PATRICIA HOPKINS
The Feminine Face of God

Ever-Widening Circles:
Women's Spirituality Today

*When a woman begins to be aware of the divine spark within,
she will soon be faced with a decision whether to honor and
trust it. . . . She is so accustomed to looking outside herself
for authority that the realization of God within is
radical and shattering. It changes everything.*

WENDLYN ALTER,
The Yang Heart of Yin

*I*t's our time. Women's time. The
feminine divine is reemerging from centuries of repression at a time
when we are sorely in need of inspiration, courage, and community. The
energy of the Goddess, of the Great Mother, of Mary and Sarah and
Esther and Hagar is palpable. You can feel it in gatherings of women both
large and small. You can see evidence of it in the marketplace, with goddess pendants, lunar calendars, and ritual supplies prominently featured
in increasingly mainstream stores. And now these energies are burgeon-
ing in the hearts of more and more regular folks as we gather together in

small circles to explore our spirituality. Women's circles are becoming a holy ground of communion with the sacred.

Before we plunge right into the hows, wheres, and whys of creating women's spiritual community, we want to provide some background information for those of you who are stepping onto this path. For those of you who have already been actively shaping the world of women's spirituality, we offer our views and want to make our assumptions and perspectives clear at the outset. Herewith, then, is our "busy woman's" treatment of women's spirituality in the 1990s.

When we mention that we are in a women's spirituality group, people ask a remarkably similar group of questions. For instance, What do you mean by spirituality? What is a spirituality group? How is it distinct from other kinds of groups? Why is it only for women? Is this a new age thing? And, what is *women's* spirituality, anyway? These are our brief answers to such important and complex questions.

What Is Spirituality?

Our definition of spirituality will be, of necessity, an in-process one. In process because we find that our understanding of spirituality is always evolving. And of course there is no way to adequately define the essentially ineffable. As Scott Peck put it in his book *A Different Drum,* "We can define or adequately explain only those things that are smaller than we are. . . . Sooner or later we inevitably run into a core of mystery." Yet there is nothing to lose in trying, as long as we remind ourselves that such "definitions" are never to be settled on for long.

Spirit comes from the Latin *spirare,* to breathe. In essence, our spirit is what animates and quickens us, what makes us alive. Spirituality, then, in our view, is the practice of staying consciously connected with what makes us alive, with our own selves, with one another, and with the Great Other.

Another aspect of spirituality is the part of us that strives to make existence meaningful. Are all these events and circumstances of our lives truly random and pointless, as agnostics and atheists would argue? Or is there some deeper design in our lives, in what happens to us, in our work, in our rela-

Spirituality is rooted in desire. We long for something we can neither name nor describe, but which is no less real because of our inability to capture it with words.

MARY JO WEAVER

Springs of Water in a Dry Land

2

tionships? Knowing at the outset that we will never have all the answers, we embark on our spiritual journeys in order to make sense of our lives.

How would you define spirituality? How has it changed since you were a child? In the last five years? We invite you to formulate your own definition. What is it, and what role does it play in your life?

What Is a Spirituality Group?

A spirituality group is a self-selected gathering of people who want to explore, express, and develop their experience and understanding of spirituality. (Of course, there can be mixed-gender and men-only groups, but this book is about women-only groups.)

You might immediately ask how these groups are different from therapy or support groups. The lines between them sometimes blur. Therapy and the recovery movement are problem oriented. Support groups focus on painful pasts and obstacles for growth. People come to these groups to get "fixed" and to heal. Having participated in therapy and support groups, we know that both are important vehicles for growth. We also know there is a distinction between these and women's circles that is subtle yet profound. (Not being clear which kind of group you want can cause problems for groups. We discuss this further in chapter 4, "Creating the Circle.") Spirituality groups, while intensely personal, don't dwell on personalities but instead explore the archetypal, even heroic, patterns and journeys of people's lives.

Spirituality is the sacred center out of which all life comes, including Mondays and Tuesdays and rainy Saturday afternoons in all their mundane and glorious detail. . . . The spiritual journey is the soul's life commingling with ordinary life.
················
CHRISTINA BALDWIN
Life's Companion

Why Are These Groups Only for Women?

Some people find it paradoxical that women have been fighting for the right to work side by side with men for decades and yet still, in the 1990s, want to sequester themselves in women-only activities. We find this quite logical. Even though women are seeking and securing power and equality on various fronts, many find they long for a feminine haven. A place where feminine values and ways of being are not just tolerated but embraced. A place to strengthen our long-forgotten and underdeveloped senses, intuitions, and ways of knowing without the presence of men.

Women's spirituality groups are safe places, free spaces, environments that foster the development of individual gifts. In our group, and in the groups of women we interviewed for this book, women continually come home to themselves. Women's circles afford an atmosphere of discovery and growth not found elsewhere in contemporary culture.

What Is Women's Spirituality?

You might now wonder, What makes women's spirituality different from any other kind of spirituality? Certainly, spiritual experience and practice are not gender specific or exclusive. Many men hold the same values and beliefs that characterize the women's spirituality movement. However, these common values and beliefs are generally more "feminine" than "masculine," according to our cultural understanding of those terms. And generally speaking, in Western culture, it is more common for women than men to hold these beliefs.

The primary characteristic of feminist spirituality is variety. For virtually every belief that one woman claims as authentic feminist spirituality, there is another woman who will assert the opposite belief but make the same claim.

CYNTHIA ELLER

Living in the Lap of the Goddess

Women's spirituality is *not* an organized religion. There is no central organization or world headquarters, there is no agreed-upon set of principles, established doctrine, written creed, or dogma. Some of us practice Wicca, some belong to spirituality groups formed inside our temple or church, some communicate on the Internet about women's spirituality, some are pagans and neopagans, and still others have a foot in both organized religion and nontraditional women's circles. Despite all our differences, groups and individuals practicing women's spirituality share several core characteristics.

We Are a Movement of Celebration

As Hemitra Crecraft and Sue King, founders of the Heart of the Goddess Wholistic Center in Berwyn, Pennsylvania, told us, "Women's spirituality is a movement of celebration, not recovery." We are engaged in reclaiming and celebrating female energy. Women's empowerment is both the ultimate goal and the path to the goal. In a way, this explains the great variety of be-liefs and practices coexisting under the same umbrella. That is, different things empower different women.

Women's spirituality groups explore each woman's connection to the divine. We draw strength and power from our female ancestors, from the goddesses, from the archetypal divine feminine, and from honoring our own sacred path in this lifetime.

Focusing on ourselves as divine beings, as part of creation, and as cocreators is incredibly uplifting to women and leads us not only to feel better about ourselves but also to become more assertive in our lives. For most of us it is a refreshing if sometimes shocking contrast to the way we were raised to see ourselves.

Our Practice Is Rooted in Real-Life Experience

And is it possible that female spirituality through the ages may have been concealed in the minutiae of domestic life rather than expressed in the grandiosity and pomposity of churches and sermons?

SUSAN GORDON LYDON,
The Knitting Sutra: Craft as a Spiritual Practice

Women's spirituality is grounded in our experience. Rather than fo-cusing on a theology that is abstract and draws its principles from an ethereal logic, we ourselves determine what Spirit means to us accord-ing to our own experience. As Diann Neu, one of the cofounders of WATER, Women and Theology, Ethics and Religion, states:

> Feminist spirituality starts with women's own search for meaning
> and encourages women to reclaim female power. It involves women's
> actualization of ourselves to be self-transcendent. It teaches
> women to exercise our own authority for our own lives. . . . It both
> recognizes and strives to develop a basic oneness with reality.

Our spirituality is rooted in the daily experience of being a woman, whether we are cultivating herbs or cooking with them, diapering a baby, giving a presentation, or dressing for a formal dance.

Women's spirituality is an active proclamation that women (and all people) are a spark of the divine and that we ourselves are the best determinants of what is meaningful in life, what is sacred, what is moral, what is beautiful.

We Share a Reverence for the Earth

We are earth of this earth, and we are bone of its bone.
This is a prayer I sing, for we have forgotten this and so
The earth is perishing.

BARBARA DEMING,
We Are All Part of One Another

We are learning to understand and respect the natural rhythms of life. We know that all life forms are interconnected, and we try to live our lives in accordance with this understanding. Some rituals and practices are drawn from ancient pagan rites in which the seasons and cycles of nature are celebrated and studied. One of our most wonderful group meetings was held in Sally's backyard under a large locust tree and a warm, full April moon. We lay on our backs and looked up at the night sky while being led in a guided meditation on our connection to the earth.

Many women's spirituality groups share an interest in the cycles of the moon and its effect on our lives. We are learning about medicinal plants and herbs that nature offers us to heal and treat ourselves naturally. We view gardening as a spiritual practice. Whatever the form, remembering our connection with nature reminds us of our place in the world. The concept of dominion over the earth, the idea that the earth exists for human exploitation, is replaced by the reverent realization of our interdependence and oneness with her.

The divorce of our
so-called spiritual life
from our daily
activities is a
fatal dualism.

M. P. FOLLETT

Creative Experience

6

We Value the Beauty and Wisdom of Our Bodies

*Our psychological being has been severed from our biological
selves for so long that we are completely cut off
from our true natures.*

MONICA SJÖÖ AND BARBARA MOR,
The Great Cosmic Mother

One thing few women in our culture escape is a powerful sense of
dissatisfaction, even loathing, of our bodies. Almost every woman we
know has a distorted view of her own body, always looking to modify,
coerce, force, and coax it into looking some other way. Put more
starkly, a recent poll of ten thousand women found that 97 percent
"hated" some or all parts of their bodies!

Women's spirituality encourages women to appreciate our bodies
whatever size, shape, color, or age. This flies in the face of all our social
conditioning. The message is that our bodies are sacred, part of nature,
and deserve to be loved and cared for as part of the divine. Bodily functions such as menstruation, childbirth, and menopause are considered
opportunities for honoring the body. We are awakening to the joys of
yoga, dance, massage, and other bodywork as ways to bring us back to
our senses, literally. The body has wisdom for us if we learn to listen to
its teachings.

We Create Our Own Rituals

*Ritual is the act of sanctifying action—even ordinary
actions—so that it has meaning: I can light a candle
because I need the light or because the candle
represents the light I need.*

CHRISTINA BALDWIN,
Life's Companion

Self-generated ritual is a common element of nearly all
women's spirituality. Ritual serves many functions, including

*The body is wiser
than its inhabitants.
The body is the soul.
We ignore its aches,
pains, eruptions,
because we fear the
truth. The body is
God's messenger.*

ERICA JONG
Fear of Fifty

7

creating a sense of community and connecting us to the divine within us. Rather than allowing others, usually men, to prescribe and preside over our rituals, *we* decide which symbols have power for us, which movements make us feel more grounded in our bodies, which words bring us strength.

Our rituals are widely divergent and are drawn from a sometimes bewildering array of disciplines and traditions—Native American, Buddhist, new age, neopagan, shamanic, African, Taoist, the occult. Individuals and groups fashion their own particular practices to suit their circumstances.

Ritual can be created for any occasion: the birth of a child, a divorce, the onset of menopause, or the first day of spring. A ritual has immediate meaning for those that create it. A woman who is pregnant and facing a breech delivery might construct a little altar on her dresser or invoke protection in a prayer in a totally different way than a woman who is about to take the bar exam. There is no orthodoxy here. Whatever the circumstance, ritual is a sacred act that we create and conduct. It is powerful for us in ways that nothing imposed on us by others could ever be.

No one can organize your perception of God better than you can. Your own sense of ritual and theater can mark every day, as well as special occasions, with the celebration of spirit. Ritual infuses your life, but the liturgy comes from within. Your body prays in its own ways, your altar is a moveable feast of images and settings.

GABRIELLE ROTH

Maps to Ecstasy

Our Ways Are Egalitarian

Whoever walked behind anyone to freedom?
If we can't go hand in hand, I don't want to go.

HAZEL SCOTT, *Ms.*

Women's spirituality groups are almost exclusively nonhierarchial. As many women psychologists have observed, power among women is conceived of and practiced more as "power with" others than as "power over" them. We believe in strength through consensus rather than through dominion.

Most women's spirituality groups rotate meeting leadership. Even though some members of the group may have skills and talents in facilitating groups, it is important that all members are given an opportunity to lead with their own unique styles. And these unique styles and methods need to be honored by the group.

At the end of each meeting, in our group, two women—we call them "mothers"—volunteer to lead the next group. These two are responsible for determining the topic, preparing for the meeting, deciding on its structure and content, and leading the meeting itself. Many diverse ways of meeting have emerged over the last three years. It is fascinating to see the different ways of approaching a subject, the unusual activities, the kinds of altars or decorations, and the facilitation styles that our group members have developed.

Other Common Questions About Women's Spirituality

Is It Practiced Inside or Outside of Organized Religion?

Contrary to what some may think, we are *not* a movement exclusively for those fed up with traditional religions. True, many of us have felt deeply wounded by the religion of our childhood and will not set foot inside a church or temple. But many others feel just as fervently that change needs to happen within the system. These women are devoting their considerable energies toward restructuring their churches and temples from the inside.

Women are changing the way churches do their business. Last year the *Washington Post* ran a story about a Methodist minister who had breast cancer. She agonized for months before finally sharing the news with her church. Finally she could no longer keep separate her personal and professional lives. Naturally, there was an outpouring of support, much of it practical, like taking turns driving her to radiation treatments and bringing meals to her family. Some male clergy might share their vulnerability like this, but it has certainly not been the norm.

What about women who have not taken the ordination route? Or who could not? In the Catholic Church, ordination has been relentlessly forbidden to women by the Vatican. Nevertheless, the Women-Church movement has sprung up within Catholicism. The goal of

Women-Church is to "reinterpret the language, symbols, and texts of Christianity to serve women's spirituality." Women-Church has subsequently reached out beyond the confines of Catholicism to women of other faiths.

Women have been the driving force behind rewriting the traditional liturgies, hymns, and prayers to make them more inclusive and less male centered. It has meant more than simply changing every *he* to *she* or some gender-neutral word. Metaphors of war and battle have given way to gentler glories.

Within Judaism, women's groups are meeting to reexamine their legacy. Women are becoming rabbis and cantors. Grown women are celebrating their bat mitzvahs. At a recent Jewish wedding in Nashville that Sally attended, her friend Julie insisted that two of her women friends sign the marriage contract, the *katuba,* traditionally a male prerogative. Her rabbi's wife, Wendy, leads a group of women exploring what it means to be a Jew and a modern woman.

Even Orthodox Jewish women are breaking ranks with tradition. The First International Conference on Feminism and Orthodoxy was held in late February 1997. Conference organizers had expected 350 attendees, but the conference was swamped with over a thousand participants. Prime among the controversial issues was that of women's prayer groups. Increasing numbers of Orthodox women are meeting together to pray, since they are not allowed to lead prayers in a synagogue when men are present. Other hot topics were domestic violence, inequities in divorce law, and work and family issues facing the "Orthodox Superwoman."

The Unitarians, always on the forefront of social trends, have developed a curriculum for women to explore prepatriarchal religion and its modern application. Inspired by the pioneering works of Riane Eisler and Marija Gimbutas, among others, *Cakes for the Queen of Heaven* is a widely used study course.

Our own women's group is a good example of this diversity. Some women, like Robin, are definitely "undoing" a wounding religious upbringing. Others, like Sally, have had fairly satisfying or neutral experiences inside their tradition and have little to undo in terms of religious conditioning. Then there are some whose religion, though not without its contra-

I make a distinction between the doctrines of the Church, which matter, and the structure invented by a half a dozen Italians who got to be pope and which is of very little use to anybody.

BERNADETTE DEVLIN

The Price of My Soul

dictions, is very important and who continue to participate both inside their tradition and outside in nontraditional groups.

What Is the Role of the Goddess?

In our time, in our culture, the goddess once again is becoming a symbol of empowerment for women, a catalyst for an emerging earth-centered spirituality, a metaphor for earth as a living organism, an archetype for feminine consciousness, a mentor for healers, the emblem of a new political movement, an inspiration for artists, a model for resacralizing woman's body and the mystery of human sexuality.

ELINOR GADON,
The Once and Future Goddess

The Goddess fervor is yet another manifestation of the resurgence in feminine energy and power on this planet. However, this does not necessarily mean that all women are literally worshiping goddesses.

The Goddess is symbol of the archetypal divine feminine. We think she is showing up so widely now because the planet needs to develop its feminine values and qualities. The Goddess is here to help us—and we need all the help we can get as we navigate these tricky seas, passing through the perilous straits of our time. Having an icon of Kwan Yin or Isis or Astarte on one's private altar may be seen as heretical by some. We foresee these statues, and others like them, on a lot more altars in the years to come as more and more people use them to evoke the divine feminine.

Having said that, not all women involved in women's spirituality find meaning in the Goddess. Many are not attracted to her as a means of developing their spirituality but may find similar comfort and inspiration in figures like Mary, the mother of Jesus, women saints, or other women found in religious writings.

The image of the Goddess inspires women to see ourselves as divine, our bodies as sacred, the changing phases of our lives as holy, our aggression as healthy, our anger as purifying, and our power to nurture and create, but also to limit and destroy when necessary, as the very force that sustains all life.

....

STARHAWK

The Spiral Dance

Is Women's Spirituality a New Age Phenomenon?

*The magical, mythological and feminine ways of dealing
with existence left behind thousands of years ago must
now be reclaimed by consciousness.*

EDWARD WHITMONT,
Return of the Goddess

Even though the women's spirituality movement may seem like a new phenomenon—a nineties thing, something the new agers dreamed up—it's not. Throughout history, women around the world have come together in circles to worship and pray, to explore their relationship to the sacred, and to celebrate the divine in the everyday.

In the last twenty-five years, pioneering archaeologists and scholars such as Marija Gimbutas, Riane Eisler, and Merlin Stone have begun to trace and reinterpret the history of the late Paleolithic and Neolithic eras of Europe and the Middle East. These scholars have unearthed compelling evidence that suggests there was a time (beginning about 27,000 years ago and flourishing 9,000 years ago) when the way humans viewed the world, and their role in it, was vastly different from the way we now view it. At that time the kinds of ideas that are now viewed as new and revolutionary were commonplace, the norm.

These Goddess-worshiping cultures shared several similar characteristics: the divine was primarily represented in female form; the cultures were earth centered, body affirming, and egalitarian; humans were viewed as part of nature, not masters of it; and the sacred and the mundane were inextricably interwoven. Sound familiar? Not unlike the core characteristics of women's spirituality that we described earlier in this chapter.

So, what difference does it make? Why does it matter that humanity's view of the sacred once focused on the feminine? We think it's important because of the way the human mind works. It is much harder for us to imagine that something is possible if we have no historical precedent for it.

It is essential that we reclaim our history because with that reclamation comes the possibility of fundamental change. Knowing that there was a time, a long time, in fact, when life for women was very different and when women's wisdom was highly valued by society makes the prospect of such a radical shift happening in our day and age much more credible and possible. Visioning is key to creating, and in order to envision, one must be able to conceive of possibility.[1] Now is the time for these "old ways" to come forth openly, to be rediscovered and reinvented for our time, to serve women serving themselves, one another, and the planet.

....

*We don't need someone to show us the ropes. We are the ones
we've been waiting for. Deep inside us we know the feelings
we need to guide us. Our task is to learn to trust
our inner knowing.*

SONIA JOHNSON,
Going Out of Our Minds

We invite you to engage with us in this conversation now that you have read this chapter. What are your thoughts, feelings, and reactions to what we've said? What do you believe spirituality is? What do you believe women's spirituality is? Do you have an affinity with the Goddess? If so, how does she show up in your life? If not, are there historical women or religious figures from whom you draw inspiration? Do you know much about your foremothers and their spiritual practices? If so, how did these influence you? If you don't know much, what impact has that had on your life?

We are not asking you to take our word on any of this. Use what is helpful, and discard the rest. Looking for and trusting the truth of your own experience—reclaiming spiritual authority and responsibility for yourself—is the essence of the practice of women's spirituality.

---

[1] The authors would like to acknowledge Sarah Fahy, our dear friend and teacher, for her contribution to our understanding of the importance of reclaiming our heritage.

A Sampler of Women's Circles

When sisters gather
and the wind/breath/spirit blows
and seeds are scattered
and nurturing happens even when we are unaware—

MARGEE[1]

An astonishing variety of women's spirituality groups is sprouting up everywhere, as if an invisible Jenny Appleseed had scattered a million seeds over our land. These seeds have fallen on fertile ground. For some of us, our ground of spiritual communion with other women has lain fallow for centuries, if not millennia. And fallow ground receives seed like no other. Women have suddenly started experiencing an enormous thirst, a deep yearning for connection with other women and a need to redefine themselves spiritually in their own image and on their own terms.

As we expanded our research outward from our own circle, we were amazed at the number of women's spirituality groups we found. In the

[1] All the quotes in this chapter, unless otherwise noted, are taken from a logbook at a women's event held July 13, 1996, at the National Cathedral entitled "Sacred Circles: A Celebration of Women's Spirituality."

course of writing this book, we interviewed women from fifteen existing groups, including African American, Jewish, and Mormon women. Most groups are unaffiliated with organized religion. Many of the women we interviewed said that the groups keep them honest. "I can't so easily make a proclamation about what I really care about to twelve other people and then trot right out and do something completely different," said one member. "I feel more accountable to myself to walk the talk. The group keeps me clearer and on track with what is most important."

We have included thumbnail sketches of different groups because they can help women contemplating joining or beginning such a group to get a sense of the rich and varied nature of women's spirituality groups. Also, we want to show ourselves to one another. So, herewith, a sampler of the groups we found. Like the samplers our great-grandmothers made, this one provides you with several examples that you might consider as you think of your own group. There are, after all, many different ways to manifest spiritual energy. Notice, as you read, which excite you, inspire you, energize you. Ask yourself, as you witness your own reactions, what about the group triggers this response in you. These reflections may prove helpful in forming and/or honing your vision for the group of your dreams.

The Youngest Group

Several brand new groups were spawned by the celebration of women's spirituality at the Washington National Cathedral event of July 1996, including the circle that Polly Meceda belongs to. All the women met at the conference and knew that they wanted to nurture and build the spirit they had discovered there. "We were all craving the energy that we had tapped into," Polly said. So they started meeting monthly on a weeknight at an Episcopalian church in downtown D.C. Polly lives in suburban Virginia, but driving into town on a weekday evening was not a major disincentive for her. The group opted to keep the meeting open for the first three months so that they could invite new members to try the

I see a finely wrought chain of tempered silver, delicate yet strong, stretching back through time, reaching deep into the earth. . . . A chain of women, each listening to each, being present to her as she waits for her self to be born, for her feeling values to come to form and to birth. . . . Woman after woman after woman, being present, as each finds her voice.

JUDITH DUERK

A Circle of Stones: Woman's Journey to Herself

16

group out. By the time of their third meeting, they had gone from three to twelve members.

The circle is made up of women of diverse religious backgrounds, ranging in age from early thirties to sixty-nine. Most are still involved in organized religion, and all of them are seeking something deeper. At their monthly meetings, the two women who volunteer to facilitate call themselves the "goddesses." For sharing, they hold a talking stick, a branch or wand passed around; whoever holds it has everyone's complete attention. When Polly was the goddess, she brought a Native American smudge stick, a tightly wrapped bundle of dried herbs that is burned to purify the energy of a gathering. She was nervous about lighting the stick and had been planning only to show it to the group, when one of the women said, "Let's go no further until we smudge." What had started as show-and-tell turned into the beginnings of a ritual. The group moved there instinctively.

Sisters in Spirit

Sisters in Spirit is a group of African American women from all walks of life searching for a greater awareness and understanding of their true divinity and God consciousness. The group started as a family gathering of sisters and cousins who wanted to come together for the sole purpose of sharing their life experiences and offering support for improving the quality of their lives. Beginning with the natural sharing of personal concerns among women, this regular family gathering became the starting point for ongoing meetings that eventually began to include other Black women in need of a Sista support group. Now the group has grown to include more friends and their relatives and is open and receptive to all women regardless of cultural and racial differences.

As Jennifer Harrison, the founder and informal leader of the group, describes it, the vision of Sisters in Spirit is to "be a forum for us as Black women to come together to reinforce our common bonds, with each other as well as women of other races and backgrounds, to unite our spirits and help each other and our families to heal. We want to hasten the

If everyone in the world could do this once a month, there would be no more war.
·············
SUSIE MILAM

17

process of empowering ourselves by seeing that the true source of our power lies within." Learning how to trust one's inner spirit for divine guidance is one of this group's predominant themes.

Sisters in Spirit is a passionate group, very committed, and very excited about the relationships and growth that they have fostered in the last five years. "Women deny themselves by trying to be all things to everyone and forgetting their own needs," says Jennifer. These women share a level of consciousness focused on self-healing, self-awareness, and self-love as they reach out to one another in support. They meet once a month on a Sunday afternoon and share a potluck meal.

What's more, they are the only group we talked to that manages to actually take weekend retreats, not just wistfully talk about going sometime. They even have a newsletter.

The women open each meeting by reciting in unison a long invocation they have all memorized, which begins, "I know that I am pure spirit. I always have been and always will be." There is no agenda for the meetings, no predetermined topic. Allowing Spirit to shape the meetings, letting things evolve, trusting that guidance will be available as needed, the group is quite spontaneous. People take the floor as the need arises. They tell their stories. Over the years, they have learned that essentially they all have the same story, with just minor variations. The group functions like an extended family.

Sisters in Spirit makes decisions collectively. There is no formal leadership structure, although people tend to look to Jennifer to lead in times of crisis or change. In the meetings, people take over the leader's role at different times. Whenever conflict arises, they come back to meditation as a touchstone to remind themselves of who they are and what they are about. According to Jennifer, this is a place with no hidden agendas and no secrets. She feels she has matured spiritually, softening her strong personality, learning to listen more intently, and really connecting with others.

One of the unique aspects of this compelling group is its commitment to staying open to new members. One of the group's core missions is to reach out to other sisters to share what the group is learning about God and the sacredness in their own lives. In a letter to her group written in 1995, Jennifer reminded her sisters of their original intention:

Sisters in Spirit must be open to other women to join us in our transformation and healing. This is very necessary in order that we may continue to grow in spirit; we must not allow ourselves to cut off our flow of love by excluding others. The source of our good is measured by our giving to others what the Creator has given to us. Each of us is blessed with many talents. Let's share and give to others unselfishly so that we may truly do God's work.

For this group, welcoming new women into their experience of love and growth is essential to their identity as a group. As they move into their sixth year together, they continue to look for ways to extend themselves to all women.

Bosom Buddies

Bosom Buddies is almost two years old and was formed when a mutual friend brought together a group of eight of "the most powerful and dynamic women she knew" to focus on achieving their personal and professional goals. Most of these women have taken courses through Landmark Education, a commercial enterprise that provides training and coaching for people committed to leading extraordinary lives. They agree that having this experience in common is significant because it provides them with a common language for effectively solving problems, working through issues, and, most important, envisioning what's possible for each member.

They meet often, every two or three weeks, at one another's homes. They begin by sharing food, prepared by the hosting member, as they do an initial go-round to check in. They then use the teachings of a spiritual text—currently, Deepak Chopra's *The Seven Spiritual Laws of Success*—to reflect on current challenges, learnings, and growth opportunities in their lives. Following this will be the evening's structured activity, planned and facilitated by a group member, which is intended to help members clarify and achieve their life goals. Once they made a large wall chart for listing group goals and actions they would take toward realizing these. On another occasion, they created a folder containing current individual goals, brainstormed ideas and resources

> *The greatest gift we can give one another is rapt attention to one another's existence.*
>
> SUE ELLEN

for accomplishing these goals, and set up a coaching structure to encourage forward movement when inevitable challenges occurred.

It's evident that this group is about getting some serious work done. But then again, they might choose to disregard the evening's agenda entirely to respond to a member's current need or to simply enjoy one another's company, celebrate a birthday, or watch *Seinfeld*.

Like the other women's circles we know, they have struggled in dealing with the inevitable conflicts. The youngest group member, Jean, is in her midtwenties and quite verbally expressive. One of the women realized that, though she loved listening to Jean, she just had to tell her that she talked too much. Bitter medicine for some, perhaps, but just the type of coaching needed for someone whose goal is to become a powerful and effective professional facilitator. Jean appreciated the feedback, though she was upset at first, and has used it to modify her behavior to listen more and speak less in both personal and professional situations.

This is an example of the rigor of this group. Members are willing to experience the discomfort of both giving and receiving constructive feedback, anchored by the commitment each has to living to her fullest. The group decided its mission was twofold: to push one another toward their self-ascribed goals, and to be there with loving arms when that is what is needed.

A Rosh Chodesh Group

N'varekh et ein ha-hayyim / matzmihat p'ri ha-gefen
v'nishzor et sarigei hayyeinu / b'masoret ha-am.
Let us bless the flow of life / that revives us,
sustains us / and brings us to this time.

SHEHEHEYANU (BLESSING FOR RENEWAL),
Four Centuries of Women's Spirituality

Rosh Chodesh is the time of the new moon, a time when in traditional Jewish culture a woman was relieved of her domestic studies. The Jewish calendar is lunar based, and in the old days the time of Rosh Chodesh was announced by the blowing of the *shofar* (ram's horn) from mountaintop to mountaintop.

In recent years, Jewish women have reclaimed this special lunar return as a time for them to meet together in small circles. Currently, thousands of Rosh Chodesh circles are meeting regularly all over the country. Arlene Ages, who started the movement, did not prescribe a set protocol for gatherings, and thus there is tremendous variety in their forms and practices. They do, however, share a common intention to explore and experience Shekhinah, the Hebrew word for "the feminine face of God."

Joanie Chase, a single, thirty-four-year-old woman, is the executive director of a thriving nonprofit educational organization in Washington, D.C., called Everybody Wins! She describes the women in her Rosh Chodesh group as being wise, warm, committed to Judaism, and emanating lots of light and hope. Joanie joined the group at its inception eight months ago. She was honored to be invited to join the group, partly because she is quite a bit younger than the other members. "Having these women in the group whom I see as very wise is extremely helpful to me. I have learned a lot from them already. And I know that they have admiration and respect for me and my experiences."

To Joanie, the group is not an answer to anything but rather a "tool to figure out where you fit into Judaism and where Judaism fits in for you." It makes her sad to see so many women reject the entire tradition, when there are "so many jewels and so much wisdom" to be learned from it. She wants to find a way to "embrace this religion which is so rich in meaning and history, yet so patriarchal." Being in the Rosh Chodesh group engenders feelings of gratitude, excitement, and hope in Joanie.

Leadership rotates monthly. Two people take responsibility for each meeting; one plans and leads, the other hosts the group at her home and prepares some light snack to serve at the end of the evening. A typical meeting would start with Hebrew prayers and songs, like the "Sheheheyanu" (included at the beginning of this story), which is the prayer for the new month. Sitting in a circle, the leader (or co-leaders) introduces the theme for the evening. The leader's role is largely that of facilitator, since the meetings are usually experiential. Sometimes the leader will offer some teaching, or maybe a reading from the Bible pertaining to the theme, before heading into the heart of the

Every blade of grass has its Angel that bends over it and whispers, "grow, grow."

· · · · · · · · · · · · · ·

THE TALMUD

meeting—time for each person to share. They almost always have some guiding questions to address in their sharing, and people are invited to respond but may certainly decline.

Joanie's group has focused on a variety of topics in its short life, including: mothers and fathers and their influence on our lives, Passover (this meeting focused on Miriam, Moses' sister, who plays an important role in the Bible as a midwife, prophetess, and leader), and meditation.

Toward the end, the group will offer healing prayers for one another, family, and friends. Before ending with a song, each woman will say one word that speaks to what she wants to manifest in her life during the coming moon cycle. After the formal part of the meeting is over, the leader offers food and the women linger to chat for a while.

"I feel the direct presence of Shekhinah when I am sitting with my group," says Joanie. "Although Judaism is thousands of years old, Rosh Chodesh helps me to see that the traditions, culture, and rituals are relevant and can bring meaning to my life."

The Magnificent Seven

The Magnificent Seven is a group of women in Seattle. Among them was our friend Christine Cranston, who had just relocated to Seattle and was seeking community. Three of the seven had attended a Barbara Sher workshop together. Out of the workshop, they created a "success team," Sher's version of a professional support group. They saw the group as a way of helping one another live the lives they love. Many, like Christine, were in transition and wanted a sense of grounding and connection.

When we interviewed them, by speakerphone from a Seattle law office, their enthusiasm for the group bubbled out from the phone.

They come from diverse religious backgrounds: one was raised a fundamentalist Christian, converted to Judaism, and now calls herself a shaman. A few were raised Catholic but are no longer practicing. Christine describes her spirituality as earth based. But once in the circle, differences dissolve as "our spirit souls recognize one another." If there is a central

I long to speak out the intense inspiration that comes to me from lives of strong women.

RUTH BENEDICT

theme for this group, it is finding their place as spiritual beings having both a corporeal and corporate experience. How can they bring spiritual principles into the workplace? Where does work fit in to living? How can they network in the sense of deepening spiritual connections to one another rather than collecting business cards at a downtown reception?

Initially they met weekly but found that they couldn't sustain that frequency, and now they convene monthly in one another's houses. Their meetings last two and a half hours. They spend the first few minutes catching up, and then they move into council-style sharing, where each woman in turn has fifteen to twenty minutes to share. As the group has developed, they have learned to recognize which woman on a given night needs more love and attention. They instinctively attend to that woman, as they offer moral and practical support to one another. At the end of each meeting the facilitator for the session leads them in a meditative exercise in which they sit in a circle holding hands. They go around the circle clockwise as each woman shares what she is thankful for and tells what she wants to bring into her life.

This is one of the few groups that we found that seems to deal fairly competently with conflict. When thorny issues surface, they just talk things through. None of the members is shy. They spend a fair amount of time on the phone with each other between sessions, and they have a hard-and-fast rule about not saying harmful things behind others' backs. Going through conflict has strengthened this group of women. One woman left because she didn't feel she was getting out of it what she wanted, she didn't share the others' expectations, and she had started to feel alienated from the others. They let her go and still feel unsettled that they didn't get a sense of closure with her.

They are most eloquent in describing the gifts the group has given them: shifts in perception, different ways of seeing, getting unstuck, knowing that they are not alone, making deep connections, and feeling a sense of being home. They even appear in one another's dreams! Members have experienced professional breakthroughs, too, but what they shared with us is more in the realm of grace than pay raises.

Most women . . . are understimulated and underchallenged. Their emotions may be overused but their minds and talents are underused. [They need] challenge and stimulation as well as love and support.

BARBARA SHER

Wishcraft

23

Authors' note: We talked to Christine of the Magnificent Seven just before this book went to press. Interestingly, the group has essentially disbanded. At first we were disappointed, and maybe a little embarrassed. (It reminded us of when a large proportion of the companies profiled in the bestselling business book In Search of Excellence *had gone bad just a few years after being touted as "Excellent." But once we talked to Christine, we realized that this group's experience lends an important message to this book. Afraid that we would hear of some ugly argument or toxic clique driving the group asunder, we were relieved to learn that the group just kind of lost its urgency for the members and they stopped meeting. There was no falling out, in fact, no problem at all. Initially, the group came together as a way to help members deal with huge transitions in their lives. By the time the group stopped meeting, all of the members had successfully weathered their transitions and were in far more stable straits than when they coalesced.*

So, the moral of this story, as far as we are concerned, is that the group met the need it was created for —it was extremely helpful to seven women in finding their way through challenging changes and creating lives that are more in alignment with each of their purposes. Groups don't have to last forever to be good. Wabun Wind, a wise and experienced Native American teacher who has formed and coached women's circles for over twenty-five years, told us that some of the most powerful experiences she has ever had in groups took place in groups that met for just one time for a clear purpose. So, if forever, or two years, seems like too long to commit, you can still create a very life-enhancing group with a time-limited life span.

The Tuesday Afternoon Prayer Group

An altogether different shoot on the branch of women's spirituality is the kind of prayer and healing group to which Sally's mother, Caroline, belongs. The group started in 1973. Initially members worked on getting clear about what they wanted to be doing in their lives and on visualizing—really seeing—their dreams come true. At one point, they were asked to pray for a friend who had cancer, and thus began their journey with healing prayer. The group is always open to like-minded, like-hearted kindred spirits. People are not asked for an ongoing commitment to attend.

The group of five or six women (depending on who is in town) gathers every Tuesday afternoon at four for an hour in Caroline's living room. They come from different faith backgrounds, sharing a common belief that words and thoughts have power and that they are part of a network of "unknown co-workers." Each keeps a little notebook of who she is praying for on a daily and weekly basis. Group members have committed to their own daily prayer practice in which they concentrate their thoughts and prayers in turn on each person on their list. When they get together, they check in and then update the group on how each person on the list is doing.

After reviewing each "case," they may add or subtract names from their lists, depending on how each is doing. Then they move into their regular ritual. The leader for the day reads a passage from a favorite book. Each leader has a slightly different approach. She then leads a meditation during which group members visualize each of the people on their daily lists, sending them light and imagining them happy and free. The group then visualizes healing light and sends it around the circle, seeing each woman there surrounded by the light. They repeat essentially the same simple ritual each week, and after twenty-four years of weekly practice, the light glows with a powerful incandescence in the hearts and souls of these women.

Absolutely unmixed attention is prayer.

SIMONE WEIL

Covenant with the Goddess

Ginny Tyson Barnes, a dyer who uses only natural sources, a weaver, and an environmental activist, describes her circle as like a wave, growing of itself and constantly changing, ebbing and flowing. The circle evolved out of a journal-writing group that met for twelve years. That group had only two rules: you had to read out loud what you wrote, and you couldn't have the kind of notebook that you could tear the pages out of ! When one of the women in the journal group died after an automobile accident, the group did a ceremony for her. They had no idea what they were doing, said Ginny, but the experience was so powerful that they knew they wanted to continue in a similar vein. And so was born their group, which has continued through the past four years.

Before each gathering, Ginny sends a handmade invitation calling the women to the circle. The first year, they met monthly and worked with Clarissa Pinkola Estés's book *Women Who Run With the Wolves*. Then they decided it was time to move on, to strike out on their own. Now they work with the wheel of the year: the equinoxes, solstices, and so-called cross-quarter days, the ancient celebrations of Imbolc, Beltane, Lammas, and Samhain. Coming from a wide variety of religious backgrounds, they all feel that this earth-based and woman-centered spirituality fulfills a deep yearning.

These are women hungry to explore the feminine face of spirituality. They consecrate the space of exploration each time they come together by casting a circle. They construct altars that change spontaneously with each celebration. They spend time in meditation. Weather permitting, they make a sacred fire outdoors. At Beltane (May 1) they jump the fire, and at Samhain (October 31) they do a ritual celebrating the end the cycle of the seasons by giving to the fire pieces of paper on which they have written everything they want to leave behind. At Lammas (August 1) they have a "feast of first grains," composed of food they have harvested from their gardens and little goddess-shaped yeast breads. At Imbolc (February 1) one year, they invoked and invited Brigid, the Celtic triple goddess. They offered each other the communion of bread and wine, saying, "Brigid would like you to have this." These simple, heartfelt, and spontaneous rituals evolve naturally out of the group's growing confidence in their own spirituality and their trust in one another.

Early on they realized that they needed some instrument or device to honor each woman's sharing. They wanted something that would help remind them to allow each woman to speak without interruption and to preserve the sense of sacred sharing. And so they fashioned a talking stick, with all women helping to decorate it. They close each gathering by passing a kiss from cheek to cheek, first going around the circle sunwise, then moonwise. As the group evolves and grows, the leadership has also begun to pass around the circle. Ginny con-

Call it a clan, call it a network, call it a tribe, call it a family. Whatever you call it, whoever you are, you need one.

JANE HOWARD

Families

siders her work with the group a reflection of her personal covenant to serve the Goddess in each of us.

*Mother Goddess is reawakening, and we can begin to recover
our primal birthright, the sheer, intoxicating joy of being alive.*

STARHAWK,
The Spiral Dance

A Group with a Vision

Another stitch in our sampler is a ten-year-old circle that currently has seven members and meets in one another's homes on the second Wednesday of each month. It is a place for spiritual nourishment, a place where the women feel free to experiment with different spiritual practices and to learn from one another. Several years ago, they spent quite a bit of time developing a shared vision for the group. Each wrote down what she wanted the group to be, and together they wove it all into a single statement to guide the group.

They have had pajama parties, have explored Sufi dancing, and have written poetry, and together they made a quilt for a home for boarder babies, children with AIDS whose parents are not able to care for them. Women take turns leading various activities. When there are no volunteer leaders because everyone is too busy, they have a potpourri meeting where everyone brings in a little snippet of something to share—a poem, a song, a prayer.

They experiment with ritual, bending their own traditions, turning a seder into a gratitude ritual. And they freely invent their own rituals and meditations to mark rites of passage, solstices, and special occasions. They are working together to claim their own individual spirituality.

*Female friendships
that work are
relationships in which
women help each
other to belong to
themselves.*

··············

LOUISE

This group has developed a process for introducing new members. They open the group once a year in the fall. For four months, the prospective member focuses on what she wants to give and to receive from the group, and the group and she focus on whether the fit is right. She also co-leads an evening with a veteran member. They then ask for a year's commitment.

Washington Family Theater Dance Company

"Do you like to dance?" Claudia Jean Hill's group started with this unlikely question in a Relief Society meeting in 1990. (The Relief Society is the name of the women's organization of the Church of Jesus Christ of Latter-Day Saints, the "Mormon" church.) Claudia had dreamed for years about putting together a women's dance ensemble to complement the community theater group she had formed six years earlier. Then she noticed a new face at the meeting. "Do you like to dance?" she asked Kelly. It turned out, in fact, that not only did Kelly like to dance, she had a master's degree in dance and was very interested in making Claudia's dream a reality.

They began meeting with eight church women, all of whom had differing degrees of experience in dance. One was an aerobics instructor, a few had performed before, and some were complete novices. Together these women formed a vision that combined community outreach and inner growth. Claudia says she "felt strongly about the church offering some wholesome things in the arts—where creative growth can flourish in a morally uplifting atmosphere and families can feel comfortable participating." Balancing the performing with the inner work of creativity and self expression, the Washington Family Theater Dance Company was born.

The thing that fascinates the two of us about this group is that though some of its practices differ from those we will recommend in chapter 3—for instance, they don't practice council sharing—the spirit and intention of the group resonate completely with those of our own group and the others we profile here. Their intention is clear—creating and performing expressive dance inside a tradition that has not previously included formal liturgical dance. This is not a group based on telling stories, at least not verbally. Though they often begin with a brief prayer, their "invocations" center on warming muscles, stretching hamstrings, and breathing full breaths. Their circle formed through the sharing of ideas for choreography and moving their bodies together. "A different kind of closeness comes from working/playing in the physical body. There is lots of vulnerability." One woman couldn't wear the unitard because she was embarrassed about her weight. "We all had to work through issues about our bodies," remembers Claudia.

Kelly served as the artistic director for the first few years, with Claudia as her behind-the-scenes partner. They rehearsed weekly and asked for regular attendance from all the women. Decisions were made primarily through consensus, with Kelly stepping in as leader from time to time. A nursery was established to care for their many young children during rehearsals. Later, when Kelly moved away, the leadership began to rotate.

Their concert choreography also extended to pieces that included teens, children, and audience participation. The goal was to enrich and educate at the same time.

Making a point to highlight the different gifts of each dancer, the group typically presents solo pieces along with ensemble ones. The solo pieces have been particularly challenging and meaningful for the dancers. When it is her turn, a woman may choose some emotional or spiritual issue she is grappling with and create a dance that depicts this inner journey. When she is ready, she asks for and receives input from the other members with the idea that giving and receiving the input is done with love. This process of dancing their innermost demons and dreams has forged a powerful bond.

When asked what her greatest gift from this experience has been, Claudia replied, "I experience a real sense of the feminine divine in myself through dance. How good and beautiful and harmonious the physical and spiritual realms can be, together in creative expression! I learned how our bodies are instruments of the spirit—not just to know that theoretically, but to experience myself as an expression of God's goodness and love."

She continued, "I also realize that it is the bond, the safety and love that grew from our work together, that allows the spiritual expression. When we do our solo dance pieces, it is with the full support of the other women. It is these friendships, so affirming and soulful, that allow each of us to grow."

Seven years later, the group, now three core members, continues to create together and to perform several times a year, mostly upon request.

On the surface, these circles seem very different. Some pray, some meditate, some ritualize, others read scripture or jump the Beltane fires. Though the forms of worship may differ, they have all been "containers of emergence" for their members. Our dancing Mormon friend, Claudia, sums up our sampling: "Being with women like this is another way of being, another way of being born. We all have imperfect mothers, but with this group, we get to mother ourselves anew. It's as if all the positive aspects of all the women combine into the Divine Mother, and we are all mothered by her in just the way we most need."

Women's spirituality groups are places for rediscovering, liberating, sparking, and nurturing all of our gifts. These groups are coming into bloom everywhere, like bright spring bulbs pushing up through the muddy spring earth—gifts to us from a generous Creatrix.

Just as with a garden, what you plant in your circle will determine, to a large extent, what you grow and harvest. This sampler shows just some of the countless ways women are planting: seeds that grow out of Judaism, Christianity, or Goddess worship, others that focus on work or social activism. Only you can know what seeds are the right ones to sow in order that your own particular plot will flower and bear fruit that satisfies your taste. Listen to your heart and sow with love.

Circle Basics

Everything the Power of the World does is done in a circle.

BLACK ELK,
Black Elk Speaks

*T*hough they take many forms, most women's circles function according to some basic principles and practices. Of course, not every group follows every one of these all the time, but the groups we know about have a remarkably similar way of functioning. So similar are they, in fact, that it is fascinating to remember that there is no central organizing body prescribing the structure. Yet these groups, many unaware of the others, have evolved to serve the women who created them.

In describing the fundamental practices of women's groups, Gloria Steinem wrote in *Ms.* magazine, "These are not rules. They are organic practices that help produce the desired results by being desirable themselves. The ends are the means." Those that use these guidelines find them to be healing and affirming in and of themselves and that their use is conducive to spiritual development.

The eight basics we offer here are the bare essentials. You may add more, and you may put your own spin on these, but we highly recommend

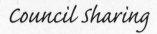

you adopt these. Of the many successful groups we have interviewed, all of them practice variations on these themes.

Council Sharing

Adapted from Native American traditions in which tribal members met in council to make decisions and solve problems for their people, council sharing is surprisingly simple. In essence, **one person at a time takes a turn speaking while the others listen.**

An essential element of this practice is the use of a "talking stick." The person whose turn it is to speak holds the stick, which gives her the authority to speak and be listened to as long as she holds it. A wise and experienced teacher and author, Wabun Wind, who contributed generously to this book, suggests that groups of women use a more feminine object in their circles, for example, a bowl. The talking bowl (or rock or doll or fruit or anything you want to use) makes it very clear who has the floor, and it eliminates interruptions and confusion.

Each person holding the talking bowl has as much time as she needs to speak to the questions of the moment. She may need to pause, she may need to search inside herself for words to express herself, but as long as she holds the bowl, the others are silent and listening. Sometimes a general idea is given of how long each person should talk. In smaller groups it might well be ten or fifteen minutes. But if a woman in our group is really sharing deeply, she is never hastened along. We have found that everyone gets as much time as she needs.

The power in council lies not only in the individual sharing, but also in the synergy generated by everyone speaking her truth. It is fine for someone to pass the bowl on to the next person without speaking. Sometimes there is nothing to say or nothing to say yet. Each person should be allowed to judge for herself when to take the talking bowl and whether to pass it without speaking at all.

Most typical conversations in our daily lives are filled with interruptions; we finish one another's sentences, ask questions that steer the subject in another direction, make comments, and state opinions about what someone is saying. None of that

Methods and means cannot be separated from the ultimate aim.

EMMA GOLDMAN

My Further Disillusionment with Russia

takes place in council. There is interaction between speaker and listener, but it is of a different nature than social conversation. In council, **there should be no interruptions while a person is talking.** It is her time. It is her voice. It is her opportunity to speak as she is moved to do. (In meetings of Alcoholics Anonymous they also observe this practice. There they refrain from "cross-talk.")

When participating in council sharing, it is wise to practice speaking from the "I." That is, **rather than generalizing about how people feel, or how women feel, or even how someone else must feel, we suggest you say how you feel, specifically.** State your experience as yours. It's the only perspective you can honestly and authentically claim, anyway. Speaking this way is bold and powerful, and it takes some getting used to, for it is not the generally accepted norm of social discourse.

Council sharing allows Spirit to speak through us. Its simple structure lends enough quiet and focus for people to listen to themselves, to speak their truths, and to be honored and supported by mindful listening. In council we "hear each other into speech." This is an unusual practice, and for many of us it may be quite uncomfortable and feel unnatural at first. We were recently leading a workshop in which we asked participants to practice council sharing. We explained the guidelines of council, and the small groups proceeded to share deeply, even though most of them had never met before this day. At the end, one woman approached Robin and asked about the council. "Was it right that we did not respond to each other during the sharing? No one commented on what people said. Was that right?" Robin told her that that was exactly the spirit of council. She then added anxiously, "But if no one responds, how do you know what to say?" Eureka! This is a core teaching of council. Trust yourself enough to allow what is there for you to say to just emerge. It may even surprise you. We don't always need to know what to say or to have a perfectly articulated idea or to have it all down pat. None of us has our lives "down pat" anyway, so why pretend that we do?

Our socialization to please others is so pervasive that it virtually takes over in the communication process, and we aren't even aware of it. We use people's questions and comments to give us cues as to what we should say next. In the process of all this people pleasing, we may completely ignore what we had to say in the first place, or we may never even have been in touch with it at all. We become entertainers, and some of us are quite skilled at this form of social banter.

Council sharing takes the entertainment out of communication. Because there are no external cues as to how people are reacting or judging what one is saying, **the guidance must come from within.** What do I want to say about this? What is true for me about this question or issue? The speaker stands alone with the truth of her own experience. In this way, council helps people to become increasingly self-referential, that is, looking inside rather than outside for direction.

Wabun Wind, who for many years trained people in creating councils, told us that one of her cardinal rules for groups was the rule of non-interference. Not only should there be no cross-talk (responding to one another, commenting back and forth), she told us, there should be no physical response to the speaker. For instance, a woman is speaking from her heart and her emotions are stirred. She is crying, maybe even sobbing. Wabun suggests that the women in the circle should not pat her, hold her, or even hand her a tissue. She points out that any of these apparently comforting actions can actually serve to shut down the emotion being expressed. As a culture, we are generally so uneasy with strong emotion that we will do anything necessary to suppress it, including comforting someone into silence. Wabun recommends no response to emotion other than intent listening.

Don't get us wrong. Council isn't always a somber experience. It can be excruciatingly funny and wonderfully light-hearted. We've heard some of the most hilarious things in council because people are at their most unguarded.

Once everyone has had a chance to share, a more typical conversation may ensue. People may comment on others' sharing and the impact it had on them. Sometimes women notice themes that emerged in the council and raise these for further examination.

To voice something you're feeling and put observations into words with another person who is totally present is a creative act embodying soul and love.

JEAN SHINODA BOLEN

Handbook for the Soul

34

Listening Without an Agenda

*Listening is a magnetic and strange thing, a creative force. You
can see that when you think how the friends that really listen
to us are the ones we move toward, and we want to sit in their
radius as though it did us good, like ultraviolet rays.*

BRENDA UELAND,
Strength to the Sword Arm

Listening is an integral part of council, and it is so important that it deserves its own section. Most of us listen with an agenda. We may not realize it, but we do. The broad agenda looks something like this: Do this person's comments confirm *my* view of the world? If so, I accept and approve of what is being said. If not, I disapprove and reject what is being said. From there, we have subagendas about getting what we want, proving our point, being right, and so on. So, we are listening for what we agree and disagree with and what we need to do next to validate or invalidate what is being said, depending upon our comfort with it. We may be nodding in what looks like tacit agreement, but underneath we are furiously and automatically scheming to get our point across and to win at the ongoing game called "Being Right."

As the anonymous author of the book *Each Day a New Beginning* stated, "How hard it is, how often, to be still and to fully listen to the words, rather than the person. How much more familiar it is to filter the message with our own ongoing inner dialogue—our own ongoing continual assessment of another's personhood at the very time our higher power is trying to reach us through them."

With all this mental activity, we usually don't really hear a thing. We think we do, but what we are "hearing" is just the cacophony of the evaluation machinery of our own minds.

In women's spirituality groups, **the role of the listener is to listen without an agenda. It is irrelevant whether or not you agree or disagree with what someone is saying. It doesn't matter whether you think she is right or wrong. What matters is that you**

*Someone to tell
it to is one of the
fundamental needs
of human beings.*

················

MILES FRANKLIN
Childhood at Brindabella

listen carefully and accept what is being said as her reality.
This is what her world looks like, this is how she feels, period, even if
you are sure that with just one small skillful remark you could set her
straight or make it all better.

There is no need for agreement in the group. People are different,
and they need to be free to express their feelings without the pressure to
conform to a norm. We all get plenty of that kind of pressure in our
families and workplaces. Here, we want to give people the space to express their true selves. Attentive, nonjudgmental listening provides the
supportive, encouraging environment needed to coax people out of
their fear of judgment and their self-protective armor.

This kind of listening can have a radical impact on people. In
the South, an organization called the Listening Project is training volunteers in this high art of listening and then sending
them out into the community to listen to people speak about
pressing social problems such as racism. Herb Walters, co-
leader of the Listening Project, describes the essence of empowering listening for change:

> We teach empathy. Empathy isn't agreement. It's
> understanding where people are starting from and seeing the
> potential. It involves listening at a very deep level so that one
> builds a relationship of trust and respect. To listen at a deep
> level you have to let go of your own strong beliefs. It's a
> spiritual process of seeking God in the other person. . . .
> When people feel safe, they challenge themselves. When you
> give people a chance to open up, they really examine their
> beliefs, and sometimes they reinvent them.

*When we don't listen
fully to each other,
when we don't revere
the Spirit within
others that's trying to
talk to us, we destroy
the connection that
wants to be made
between Spirits.*

....

ANONYMOUS

Each Day a New Beginning

Listening without an agenda also means that you are not there to
solve problems or make interpretations for people. So often, in an attempt to be helpful, we suggest options and actions to solve others'
problems. However, this is not the purpose of council listening. In fact, it
is antithetical to it. When the listener offers solutions and makes interpretations, she invariably puts her spin on things. The speaker is then
prompted to respond to the spin, and the conversation (which it has become at this point) careens away from the inner truth that comes from
solely listening to what emerges from the speaker.

Scott Peck puts his finger precisely on this point in his book about community building, *The Different Drum:*

> Paradoxically, then, a group of humans becomes healing and converting only after its members have learned to stop trying to heal and convert. Community is a safe place precisely because no one is attempting to heal or convert you, to fix you, to change you. Instead, the members accept you as you are. You are free to be you. And being so free, you are free to discard defenses, masks, disguises; free to seek your own psychological and spiritual health; free to become your whole and holy self.

This runs counter to all of our training. As women, we are there to comfort, to make things better for those we love. In council sharing, we are there to listen . . . period. **Council also means that while you are listening, you are not planning what you are going to say when the talking bowl is passed to you.** You are 100 percent present for the person who is speaking. Native Americans believe that council is a sacred practice and that Spirit works through council if people create an open and willing channel for it. We have experienced council magic many times.

With the gift of listening comes the gift of healing.
....
CATHERINE

DE HUECK DOHERTY

Poustinia

There is no need to plan and no one to impress. Just take the talking bowl when you feel ready, and begin to speak. As long as you are speaking your truth, what could be wrong? In wanting to look good to others, we plan what we are going to say, withdrawing our attention from the person who is talking. Premeditation stifles Spirit. Trust allows Spirit to voice itself. Listen when it's time for listening, and speak when it's time to speak. See what happens. It's all about allowing rather than controlling.

Rotating Leadership/Shared Ownership

There is no single savior being awaited. Rather, the savior is spread out among us, emerging from each of us as we bring forth the fruits from our sacred garden into our daily lives. It is we who must save us.

SHERRY RUTH ANDERSON AND PATRICIA HOPKINS,
The Feminine Face of God

Patriarchal ways have strongly conditioned our ideas of leadership. The "normal" expectation is that there is one leader. That leader has the responsibility for getting people going, for keeping the ship afloat. It's a military model, which might work in wartime (although even that is being called into question), but it is a model that women's spirituality has outgrown. Nevertheless, it was probably the model that most of us were raised with by our captain-fathers.

No doubt this hierarchical model is expeditious and efficient. But is that what we are really after here? *No!* There is no virtue in expedience in this setting. We are not running a skirmish or a maneuver. We are growing souls. And there is nothing more antithetical to this tender process than traditional leadership, where most of the power resides in one person. In some respects, hierarchy is a familiar and comfortable place for us to be. But it is not a nurturing place.

Rotating leadership allows everyone in the group to take the group in her own direction when her turn comes. This can be confronting to people. Those whose second nature it is to pick up the ball and run with it or to take over any situation and organize it may find it hard to sit back and rest with a leader who is unfamiliar with the role, who may be awkward, or who just plain does it differently. By contrast, those who would normally blanch at the thought of leading anything may have to stretch to step into the limelight and expose themselves by leading. After four years, two of the people least comfortable with leading led our meeting last week. Remembering how tentative and halting they had been in previous meetings, we marveled at their ease and command of the situation. Their leadership was seamless. Rotating leadership is a journey out of comfort and into growth.

Sharing the leadership means sharing the investment and ownership in the group. If the same people do all the work and are always out in front, it becomes, by default, their group. The others are merely along for the ride. Thus it is important to monitor the leadership, spreading it out consciously to ensure against negative dynamics and power grabs.

The best way to do this, we have found, is to have a different pair of "mothers" volunteer to facilitate each meeting. It's up to them to plan the agenda, notify the other group members, and make any arrangements beforehand. Once a year or so, usually in the summer, we have a "motherless" and totally spontaneous meeting. At various times, group members have volunteered to do other things as well, like organizing special outings (we all went to see Marianne Williamson together and Thich Nhat Hanh, the Vietnamese Zen Buddhist meditation teacher) or organizing family gatherings or updating the group list. We have never had the all-too-familiar situation of the majority of work falling upon the beleaguered and often resentful volunteer.

So how do decisions get made? The answer is by consensus. People decide together, by each weighing in on the matter at hand. There is no majority rule, no voting. People talk things over, and the group eventually aligns. All the groups we interviewed practice consensus decision making, and none of them has ever had any real difficulty in making decisions.

Confidentiality

The degree of individual growth that occurs in a group is contingent upon how much intimacy develops. In turn, that intimacy depends on trust. People must feel they are treated with respect and are valued by the others. One of the essential elements of trust is knowing that what you say in the group will not be repeated outside the group.

If the group is functioning well, people will share very sensitive and fragile parts of themselves as part of the growth and healing process. In our group people have disclosed experiences with incest, violence, and sexual misconduct. We all needed to know that what we shared would stay in the group. Very simply, group members must agree to maintain confidentiality regarding the contributions of other group members. This does not restrict anyone from describing her own group experience to anyone she chooses. It does restrict people from sharing what someone else said with anyone—including another group member who might not have been present at the meeting in which something intimate was shared.

Of course, **confidentiality precludes indulgence in any kind of gossip,** during or after meetings, about anyone in the group at any time. Think about the last time you found out that someone was talking negatively about you to someone else. How did you feel? Like being more or less open and

Communities have sometimes been referred to as leaderless groups. It is more accurate to say that a community is a group of all leaders.

....
SCOTT PECK

The Different Drum

39

vulnerable toward the person? You probably felt hurt and maybe even angry. Most likely the incident did not engender trust in your relationship with that person. And what about when you have been the "talker" and someone overheard you say something negative about her? Once such a breach of trust has taken place, effort is required for the relationship to get back on track and for the person gossiped about to feel trusting again. In short, **if you have something to say about someone in your group, say it to her face or not at all.** If you learn to practice this kind of discipline in your group, it will probably spread into the rest of your life as well.

Taking Responsibility for One's Own Needs

Nothing strengthens the judgement and quickens the conscience like individual responsibility.

ELIZABETH CADY STANTON,
The Women's Column

In order to avoid the codependent you-should-have-known-I-didn't-want-to syndrome that happens so often, particularly among women, people who join the group should agree to take responsibility for their own needs. For example, the group may decide to do something that one member doesn't want to do. Declining to participate in an exercise, ritual, or topic, for any reason, is perfectly acceptable. But the whole group does not have to change its plan.

Another example would be a situation where one person is experiencing a severe crisis and feels the need for the attention and support of the group. A few years ago, Laura came in and began the group by telling us that she had just found out her father had cancer. She broke into tears and asked if we could take a few minutes before going into the planned agenda to focus on her situation. We were, of course, glad to oblige. The key point here is that **members ask for what they need rather than expecting the group to know and respond appropriately in all situations.** Hey—assum-

Co-dependence [is] taking someone else's temperature to see how you feel.

LINDA ELLERBEE

Move On

ing others "should just know" doesn't work in families, it doesn't work in marriages, and it doesn't work in groups. Taking responsibility for one's own experience *does* work.

Self-Reflection

Witnessing oneself is an integral part of being truly conscious. The same is true of conscious groups. **Successful women's circles, like all true communities, must be able to step back and observe themselves.** How are we doing? Are we still having fun? Are the individuals in this group, for the most part, growing? Are we acting in alignment with our intention?

A day-to-day awareness is needed for a group to remain healthy. Members need to speak up with their perceptions about their own and the group's functioning whenever concerns arise. A few months ago, Robin noticed that our group seemed to be sliding away from council sharing. Instead of one person sharing at a time, there was more and more banter and cross-talk throughout the meeting. Writing this part of the book had made Robin more mindful of the benefits of council, and she was disturbed about the trend. Robin raised this issue, voiced her observation, and stated that she would prefer keeping council in a more disciplined way. A candid discussion ensued. Since then we have been more conscious about the way we structure the meetings.

There is also a need for a more comprehensive and time-consuming type of reflection. We recommend that groups schedule at least one meeting per year to review and assess themselves. Chapter 9 offers some suggestions for questions you can use during such a process. Both kinds of ongoing monitoring enable groups to self-correct, making adjustments in style and substance as they go along.

Focus on Spiritual Development

The overall intention of any women's circle is to focus on and foster the members' spiritual development. This becomes the touchstone for everything that

When death approaches, the co-dependent sees someone else's life flash before her eyes.
....
ANNE CAROLYN KLEIN
Meeting the Great Bliss Queen

41

happens. What do we mean by spiritual development? Let's go back to our definition-in-process of spirituality: the conscious connection to what makes us alive—to ourselves, one another, and the Great Other. So spiritual development is anything that deepens or broadens that sense of connection, anything that helps us to become clearer about our own individual way of channeling Spirit through us and onto the planet. When we grow spiritually we find meaning in what once looked like chaos. On the other hand, we may also find questions where we once thought we had things all figured out. In the book *The Spiral Path,* Chandra Patel states, "Spirituality is basically our relationship with reality." Spiritual development, by definition, changes our relationship with reality. We become more alive as our connection with what makes us alive grows. We become clearer about who we really are.

The outward signs of spiritual development look different in different people at different times. Bettie is taking a calligraphy class. Laura is becoming a yoga therapist. Antoinette is taking a parenting course. Lois let herself be cared for while she was ill. The other Laura left a hellish job. Jeanne choreographed a musical. Robin and Sally are writing a book together.

Notice that pain, discomfort, and anxiety appear in these scenarios as well as joy, freedom, and serenity.

Using spiritual development as a touchstone for all that is done in the circle requires reflection and discernment. It requires routinely asking questions like: Is this ritual ultimately aimed at people connecting deeply with themselves? Is this topic likely to move people deeply? Will people be expanded?

Maintaining the focus on spiritual development helps keep the behavior of the group in alignment with its purpose, thus preventing the group from straying off in a tangential direction. For instance, if the group finds itself spending several meetings in a row talking about one person's issues, asking the question about the purpose of the group could be useful. People may realize that the group has leaned too far in the direction of a therapy or support group and can then redirect the group's attentions for the next session. Another pitfall to avoid is getting too loose with bantering and chitchat. When we see

Truth is the only safe ground to stand upon.

ELIZABETH CADY STANTON

The Woman's Bible

each other only once a month, there can be a lot to catch up on. It's all too easy and certainly fun to engage in excited chatter as we reconnect with one another. So in our group we start our meetings at 7:30 but urge members to come at 7:00 for the catching-up part.

Though broadly defined, spiritual development as an organizing focus keeps the integrity of the group intact. When, Goddess forbid, your group begins to feel more like a cocktail party than a "container of emergence," check out your focus on spiritual development.

Commitment

The moment one definitely commits oneself then Providence moves too. All sorts of things occur to help that would never otherwise have occurred. A whole stream of events issues from the decision, raising in one's favor all manner of unforeseen incidents, meetings, and material assistance, which no man would have dreamed would come his way.

GOETHE

You are creating community when you form a circle. It is not a casual endeavor. For some defined portion of time, you are agreeing to enter into an unusual and profound relationship with one another. You are creating what the poet Rumi called "a community of spirit." **Powerful community is the result of both shared intention and commitment—the *c* word. You've got to have it, or the group won't sustain itself.**

Commitment, like in a marriage, means agreeing to be together and to make the group a priority above most others on the times that it meets. In good times and bad. When people aren't there, they call and check in. There is an accountability to one another and to oneself to show up. We don't stay away when we are feeling down or when an uncomfortable dynamic has surfaced in the group. Even more reason to show up.

People are going to miss meetings. Work and family crises occur, people get burned out and just can't do another thing.

The Truth does not change according to our ability to stomach it emotionally.
....
FLANNERY O'CONNOR

The Habit of Being

43

It happens. However, underlying all specific incidents of absenteeism is the commitment to be in the group. We have, in effect, taken a vow, a vow that says, "I am part of this whole. I choose this."

There is no perfect amount of time for people to commit to. Generally, the longer the time frame, the deeper the relationships will grow. However, if your group has only six months and you want to go for it, go ahead. Groups have been known to bond indelibly in one day, under the right conditions. The key is to agree to a specific time commitment and for everyone to honor that commitment. The time period can always be renegotiated and/or extended.

. . . .

So these are some of the ways a women's spirituality group is different from a coffee klatch, a team meeting, or the PTA. When forming a new group, we recommend you build these tried-and-trues in from the beginning. If your circle is having some trouble, you might want to incorporate these guidelines and see if things improve. We offer no guarantees, but we think you will be satisfied with the results. If not, talk to your sisters in another circle. Find out if their experience can benefit yours.

*Commitment is the
willingness to stick
with your vision
throughout the
inevitable ups and
downs that occur.*

. . . .

GAIL STRAUB

AND DAVID GERSHON

Empowerment

4

Creating the Circle

*It is up to us
to re-enchant this planet earth.
Up to us to midwife
at our own rebirth.*

WILL ASHE BACON

*T*his chapter is for those of you who have a strong interest in beginning a group of your own. You are ready to take the plunge and convene or join a group. We'll share the model we have developed and give you some ideas, questions, and suggestions. But the first thing to emphasize is that you already possess all the resources needed to initiate a successful women's spirituality group. Trust yourself and your intuition to guide you in creating the kind of group that you are longing for. This is not the domain of academics and clerics. It belongs to us. We are all the experts! We have sat in enough meetings, whether at work or at our kids' schools, our temples, or our churches, to know the difference between what deadens the soul and what gladdens the heart.

We started our group with such a sense of delighted expectation that we had little room for anticipating problems. Call it naive or beginner's mind, but we didn't encounter many stumbling blocks. However, although many women wanted to join our group after hearing about it, hardly any volunteered to start one on their own. We couldn't figure out why, so we started asking around.

In general, we found that people felt they needed some sort of model as well as some words of guidance from those a little farther down the path. Perhaps they were familiar with the old consciousness-raising group model and knew they didn't want that. Or they felt they were required to be experts in the domain of women's spirituality. Our response to these women was that life itself provides us with an advanced degree, but only for those who claim it as theirs.

As we became evangelists for women's spirituality groups, sharing the delight that our group has given us, we began asking ourselves questions. What would we have found helpful when beginning our group? Knowing what we know now, would we have done anything differently? Why are some evenings so much more deeply nourishing than others? We have evolved a wonderfully satisfying experience with our current group, and so we have tried to distill the essence of what has made our group such a delight. The next few chapters present the model for starting and sustaining women's spirituality groups that has evolved out of our own experience.

Our suggestions are offered as a word to the wise. When we started our group, we were winging it. Although we both had years of experience in group dynamics and leadership, we had not thought out many of the points that we raise now, nearly four years later. Nevertheless, things in our group worked out beautifully. So there is no special secret formula you must have or your group will flounder and fail. However, a few basic guidelines, in our experience, will increase the likelihood of your success.

Empower me
To be a bold
participant,
Rather than a
timid saint
in waiting . . .

TED LODER

Wrestling the Light

Find a Partner

We started our group together, in partnership, and we recommend finding a partner to help start the group for several reasons. First, you can talk through all the questions posed in this chapter and form a distinct, shared intention. The interplay of your ideas and energy will form the kernel, the seed of the group. Second, you will have different sets of friends, contacts, and pools of potential group members. The makeup of the group will be broader and will have more diversity. Third, even in the first meeting, you and your partner can model some of the basic group guidelines, like shared leadership. Rather than looking to one person as the leader in the first couple of meetings, people will begin to see how shared leadership works.

And, last and most important, having a partner is the best antidote for discouragement and self-doubt, in the highly unlikely event that only a few women show up at the first meeting or someone tries to sabotage your efforts through jealousy or ignorance. It's always more fun to have a buddy to work with, too.

Once the group is formed, your role(s) as convener of the circle will fade, and hopefully you will become no more or less prominent than any other member of the group. However, at the beginning, you have a very important role: to articulate the call and to be a beacon shining forth, showing the way to a circle of feminine power and possibility.

Form Your Intention: What Do You Really Want?

What kind of group do you want? What is the purpose of the group? What are you seeking from the group? The first thing you will need to clarify is your intention for the group. The more clear and explicit your intention is, the more compelling your message will be as you begin to gather members. Women will self-select based on the signal you are transmitting about what you want to create. The clearer your intention, the better able they will be to decide, in advance, if there is a match between their interests and yours.

Much as if you were planting a garden, first you must decide if you want vegetables or flowers. Then what kind of plants—shade loving or sun loving. Envisioning your garden before you buy your seeds will help you to cultivate just the kind of beauty for which your heart yearns. So, for instance, if you just announce that you want to start a women's spirituality group and you invite people to a meeting, you may find you have convened a group of people who really don't belong in the same group. One person may want to focus on writing or another form of artistic expression, one may want to study

How precious small women's groups are at this time when we are just beginning to trust the truth of our experience.

. . . .

SHERRY RUTH ANDERSON
AND PATRICIA HOPKINS
The Feminine Face of God

scripture, and another may be looking for a book group. Planting flowers that need very dry soil right next to those that need lots of water is not going to sustain the health of either kind. Plus, it will drive you crazy! Likewise, starting out with a lot of different agendas will not lead to a very cohesive group.

Clarifying Your Intention: What Kind of Garden Do You Want to Grow?

As soon as we believe in our vision we find ourselves attracting the worldly "nutrients" we need to have our mental seed grow to fruition.

GAIL STRAUB

AND DAVID GERSHON

Empowerment

To assist you in selecting your seeds, we offer the following questions to consider. In responding to them, let your intuition, your inner voice, be your guide. Let go of any "shoulds" or predetermined ideas of how you are supposed to do it, and follow your heart. For instance, having been raised by civic-minded parents, Robin would have found it easy to focus our group on doing good deeds in the world. It was only by listening to her inner voice that she was able to discern that this was not the direction for her, at least not initially. She wanted to focus more on inner growth. You, too, may be surprised with the answers you find.

In determining your intention, ask yourself these questions:

- What is calling you to do this? What has prompted you to want to start a group?

- What kind of a group do you want for yourself?

- Do you feel drawn to affiliate with an existing organization, temple, or church? Why or why not?

- If you do want to affiliate, what form will that affiliation take? (This could be anything from renting meeting space to obtaining official recognition.)

- Do you want people to share a similar faith tradition or perspective, for instance, Judaism, Christianity, Goddess worship? Or do you prefer that people have more diverse faiths?

- Is it to be primarily a sharing and nurturing kind of group, providing a place to explore the sacred for its members? Or do you envision the group's primary purpose as taking action in the world?

- Do you want to focus on one aspect of spirituality, such as creativity, book study, or service?

- What kind of commitment are you willing to make? Six months, a year, more?

- What are your requirements for satisfaction in a group? What's a must? What would be nice to have but not critical?

- What are you seeking to avoid in a group experience? Why?

Put Out the Word

Once you begin to clarify your intention, start talking about it. But a word of caution here. Be discriminating about the people you choose to discuss this with. Many people may be interested, but some may be threatened or downright hostile. Some will feign interest to be polite. If your intuition warns you not to share about the group with someone, heed it! You will be protecting yourself and the embryonic group from suspicion, ridicule, or fear.

You may want to write out your intention in the form of a letter. Writing often helps to fine-tune our ideas and inner stirrings. The letter could be used to invite people to the group. People's responses and questions will help you find your way to even greater clarity. People may ask questions like, "What do you mean by spirituality?" "Why are only women invited?" "What is women's spirituality anyway, and how is it different from men's spirituality?"

There is no one right answer to any of these questions; however, you may want to think about them as you prepare to invite members into the group. Don't be discouraged as you encounter these questions. Women's spirituality groups are definitely threatening to the status quo. People sense this, and their cautionary curiosity will often be disguised in challenging questions.

Sally was on an airplane recently, returning from a wedding in California. The man next to her noticed that she was reading a book called *Arching Backward,* by Janet Adler. He asked Sally about the book, and they quickly got into a discussion

Manifesting a vision is not static and definitely not linear; rather, it is an organic process of adapting and changing as we interact with many unknowns. A seed planted in the ground automatically adjusts as it interacts with rocks, roots, poor growing conditions, infertile soil, and so on. This is the way of growth and manifestation.

GAIL STRAUB

AND DAVID GERSHON

Empowerment

about women's spirituality. Now this was a friendly, curious guy, not at all hostile. But he couldn't help wondering, he commented at one point, if men hadn't set up the social guidelines the way they are solely to protect their women and children! Good point, Sally answered, and then she calmly proceeded to offer her point of view, to which he respectfully listened.

A few years ago, Sally would have never have had the equanimity and patience to engage in this kind of dialogue with him. As you talk with people about your intention for a group, you will gradually become more comfortable with these kinds of encounters. In fact, the strangers are the easy ones. It's the husbands and fathers and friends that will really get you!

Whom to Invite

Once you have formed your intention, you will be ready to begin inviting people to join your group. We do not recommend the bulletin board approach—putting up a notice announcing the formation of a group. This is not a "see who shows up" potluck affair but rather a precious and sacred opportunity to create spiritual community. Don't take this lightly. The decisions you make as to whom to bring into the group are *very* important. Ask for spiritual guidance in whatever way works for you. Use prayer, meditation, or any other tool that helps you discern direction.

We have used one method of receiving guidance several times in writing this book. And you can use this on any issue you are mulling over in your life. Write down a question regarding your issue on a piece of paper. For instance, "Is Sandy the right person to invite to be in our group?" Before you go to sleep, read the question, put it under your pillow, and ask for guidance. Be very attentive to your dreams, and notice your first thoughts upon waking in the morning. If you are asking the right question, you will very likely receive some intuitive direction. If you don't receive an answer, even a subtle leading, try rephrasing the question and doing it again.

Trusting our intuition often saves us from disaster.

....

ANNE WILSON SCHAEF

*Meditations for Women
Who Do Too Much*

Here are some suggestions for choosing your people:

Choose only psychologically stable people. A spirituality group is not a therapy or support group. We have nothing against group therapy, but in a spirituality group you don't want to spend most of your time and energy working on people's personal problems. Women's circles are not havens for "victim consciousness." Psychologically stable people still have problems, but they are not "cases," or what Julia Cameron calls "crazymakers" (in her fabulous book, *The Artist's Way*). That is, they don't spend the majority of their life energy in crises that require lots of emotional resources. This is not to say that crisis is bad; we've both been through stages of our lives when we were "cases," too. But this is not the kind of person who will do well in a group focused on spiritual development.

Choose different kinds of people. Diversity is one of the key elements of a stimulating and growing group. When we asked our members to reflect on what they learned most from being a part of the group, many of them said that being in intimate relationship with women so different from themselves had been very broadening for them. Having some women in the group who would not ordinarily be in our lives is extremely valuable. It allows us to see the world through their eyes and to see possibilities and realities we would not otherwise see. So, when considering differences, include the following: race, socioeconomic status, sexual orientation, geographical background and national origin (Southerners, Northerners, people raised or born in other countries), religious preferences and backgrounds, temperament (mystics and activists), and generation. This last difference has been the richest for our group. We range in age from the midthirties to the early sixties.

Don't invite people because you think you should or because you owe them. Be very mindful when offering invitations. This is not a one-time party but a circle that will meet regularly, will get to know one another intimately, and will grow to be part of one another's lives over a period of years, perhaps decades. Before you invite someone to join, see if you can imagine sitting in a circle with her, telling her something important about yourself, and listening to her heartfelt concerns. If this kind of fantasy stands the hair up on the back of your neck or makes you cringe, look a little further. Is this really someone you want to invite? Be clear that this person is right for the group before you extend an invitation.

Crazymakers are those personalities that create storm centers. . . . Charismatic but out of control, long on problems and short on solutions. Crazymakers like drama.

JULIA CAMERON

The Artist's Way

You will likely find, using this simple criteria, that some people you consider to be friends are just not making the list. A person may have too many problems, you may have too much emotional baggage with her, or you just don't trust her enough. Not everyone you like will be appropriate for your group. Likewise, you may know people you do not consider close friends with whom you can readily imagine sharing the circle. Use and trust your intuition. This is one of the rare opportunities for you to envision and fashion a group of women for your own nurturance.

Invite enough people so that you end up with between five and fifteen members. Some of the people you invite may decide to opt out after the first meeting. Smaller groups foster more intimacy and time for personal sharing. Leadership will be a more frequent responsibility in the smaller group, since the lead role rotates each meeting. Larger groups provide more stimulation from different kinds of women with different styles, but more attention has to be placed on making sure everyone has time to share. Do you have a preference for small or large groups? Keep that in mind, and invite accordingly.

Once you have formed the group, leave it open for the first three months. When you develop and put out a powerful intention, it's important to pay attention to who shows up. It may not be just the usual suspects and reliable friends. Leave room for the unexpected. For this reason, we recommend leaving the group open for three months before closing it. This represents a departure from our group's experience. We closed our group to newcomers from the beginning, since sixteen women showed up at our first meeting and all wanted to stay involved.

Numbers permitting, it is appropriate to have new women come try out the group for the first few meetings. You can all decide if the group is a fit. Building trust and intimacy are critical to the successful coalescing of the group, and they are harder to develop when the group is in flux initially. But you will have plenty of time for this deeper work and bonding. New people can also seem distracting, since they have to be brought up to speed and their presence brings a different energy into the group. But some groups find that the new blood

There is an "allness" to community. It is not merely a matter of including different sexes, races, and creeds. It is also inclusive of the full range of human emotions. Tears are welcome as well as laughter, fear as well as faith.

SCOTT PECK

The Different Drum

is worth the disruption, and they open their groups to newcomers each year for a few months.

Don't be surprised if nearly everyone you invite accepts!
What are *your* criteria for group members?

1. _____

2. _____

3. _____

4. _____

5. _____

Make a list of everyone you can think of who you might want to join your circle:

1. _____

2. _____

3. _____

4. _____

5. _____

6. _____

7. _____

8. _____

9. _____

10. _____

11. _____

12. _____

13. _____

14. _____

15. _____

16. _____

17. _____

18. _____

19. _____

20. _____

Extend the Invitation

Whether written or verbal, your invitation to come to the first meeting of a newly forming women's circle is a little like asking someone out on a date. That may have less than pleasant connotations, especially for those introverts among us. But don't be scared! We promise that the invitation, even if not accepted, will be received with interest, curiosity, and respect by almost everyone. Many women told us they were grateful that someone was finally organizing a group and that they had been longing for one but were too shy to start one themselves.

When inviting someone, you don't need to go into a long explanation of what to expect. After all, you aren't sure yourself at this point! Simply say that you are inviting some women to meet together to see if they want to join a group to nurture themselves spiritually. If, at this point, you have a clear intention for the kind of group you want to create, you might share this, too. But we advise you to stay open to outcome. If, as is so often the case in this age of answering machines, you have to leave a message, we recommend that you wait for them to respond to you. Don't call back if you don't hear from them right away. You want people who are truly interested, not ones who don't want to hurt your feelings by declining an invitation.

. . . .

When a group is consciously and lovingly called into being by women who are clear in their intentions and straightforward in their actions, a strong force for healing and change is unleashed. There is power and magic when women come together like this. The energies ripple outward from the simple circle, extending to the rest of our lives and going forth in time into the lives of our children and the generations beyond.

5

First Meetings

Nourish beginnings, let us nourish beginnings.
Not all things are blest, but the
seeds of all things are blest.
The blessing is in the seed.

MURIEL RUKEYSER,
"Elegy in Joy," The Green Wave

*O*nce you have clarified your intention and invited potential members, it's time to start planning your first meeting. In some ways, the first few meetings will be different from any of the others. For one thing, the people may not know each other, so some introductory icebreaker exercises are appropriate. For another, the group will have some very basic material, central to its healthy functioning, to discuss and decide upon.

Planning Your First Meeting

The way the first meetings are conducted will model how later meetings should be conducted. We recommend that you use the practices and principles of "Circle Basics" in chapter 3 in the first meeting: share the

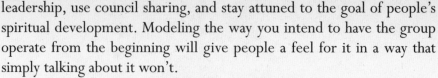

leadership, use council sharing, and stay attuned to the goal of people's spiritual development. Modeling the way you intend to have the group operate from the beginning will give people a feel for it in a way that simply talking about it won't.

With a sense of what to expect, people will then self-select for the group. That is, if they generally are in alignment with you and your intended way of going about it, they will choose to stay. If, however, they can't live with any one of these things, they will opt out. In other words, give them as much of a taste of what you have in mind as you can so that they can make an informed decision.

It's easy to get into trying to charm people into the group. Unconsciously, you may believe it validates you if they decide to join because you have been so darn appealing. *Beware!* This is that sneaky little codependent inside of you at work: "If she chooses to be in my group, I must be good." How many of us have stepped right smack in this trap in our love relationships? "If I can just snag him or her, then I must be all right." Then you get the person, and you're not right for each other, and it's hell. Who needs it? Not the people who come to your first meeting. So let's get this straight. You are a divine being. Period. Your intrinsic worth is not in question.

The real question is: Who wants to form a group in alignment with your intention and run according to the principles that are "must haves" for you? You want only the people who fit well with your goals. People are quite capable of deciding what is right for them. Trust their judgment to accept or decline your invitation. In the long run, you'll all be better off for it.

Don't be surprised if you feel anxious about the evening as you await the ring of the doorbell. You've stuck your neck out. There is no guarantee. You are trying something new. It takes guts. Will anyone want to play?

This is another one of those times that having a collaborator, partner, or friend is very helpful. Before the guests arrive those first few meetings, you can center yourselves with a brief meditation. Sit quietly facing each other. Perhaps light a candle. Breathe deeply. Close your eyes. Begin by taking turns telling each other your fears about the evening. "I am afraid no one will come." "I am afraid no one will be interested in what we are interested in." "I am afraid I'll appear very foolish in describing our vision for the group." "I am afraid to talk in front of the group." Whatever your fears are, speak them. Lay them on the table, no matter how silly they may seem. They may even sound kind of funny when you say them out loud. Once you name your fears, they will start to dissipate.

When you've emptied out your fears, state your intention for the group and for the evening specifically. For instance, "Our intention is to begin a women's circle tonight. We ask that those who are to be with us come and decide to join. We ask that those who are not right for the group at this time know that and decline the invitation. We ask that the greatest good for all be served."

This kind of centering and coming back to the intention is extremely helpful. When we give a workshop or teach, we begin this way. Of course, you can do this on your own as well. By the time you have finished, you are likely to be more calm, clear, and open to outcome.

We are always afraid to start something that we want to make very good, true and serious.

BRENDA UELAND

Me

Suggested Format for a First Meeting

In this section we offer you a loose agenda to work with in planning and conducting your first meeting. Obviously, you should only use what seems natural and intuitively right for you, and leave the rest.

1. Prepare the space. Pull the cushions or chairs into a circle and create an altar to mark the center point. This could be as simple as a candle or as elaborate and beautiful as you have time for and feel inspired to create. Play some soothing, quiet music at a low volume. We recommend Peter Kater and Carlos Nakai's *Migration* album, Flesh and Bone's *Skeleton Woman* album, or some quiet flute or chanting. See the resource guide, "Circle Resources," for more ideas. You may want to burn some subtle incense or diffuse some essential oils. You are creating a special and sacred environment, one that not only puts people at ease but also says "this is a place where we are going to share our deepest yearnings."

2. Open with a few minutes of collective silence and stretching. As a way of entering the sanctuary of the circle, begin the meeting with a few moments of closed-eye silence. If you choose, you could also lead a few simple neck and head stretches and long, slow deep breaths. This helps people to become more aware of the present moment, letting go of other concerns of the day. The opening does not have to be elaborate or eloquent; you don't need to be a yoga teacher to lead this. In fact, the more genuine and down-to-earth it is, the more people will relax and use the time to center themselves. Make it simple; use your own words.

3. Inspirational reading. Choose a reading that evokes your vision of the group or your calling toward spirituality. We often use poetry; Rumi, Mary Oliver, Marge Piercy, and May Sarton are some of our favorites. There are a few wonderful anthologies of spiritual poetry and prose in the Circle Resources.

Many of our favorite quotes are already woven here and there into this book. Here are a few more suggestions that we like:

> At first people refuse to believe that a strange new thing can be done, then they begin to hope it can't be done, then they see it can be done—then it is done and all the world wonders why it was not done before. (Frances Hodgson Burnett, *The Secret Garden*)

> I think women's spirituality today at this time is like the life you find teeming in tidal pools in the shallows of the oceans. Once that life takes hold, the sea anemones and tiny crustaceans, the starfish and the plankton, find their own food and their own means of protection. They can sustain their own lives. But in the beginning, life in the pools is fragile and must be protected from just developing, just finding our way, and we need deep, quiet, safe places in which to do this. (Carol Callopy, in *The Feminine Face of God*, by Sherry Ruth Anderson and Patricia Hopkins)

> What in your life is calling you?
> When all the noise is silenced,
> the meetings adjourned,
> the lists laid aside,
> and the wild iris blooms by itself
> in the dark forest,
> what still pulls on your soul?
>
> In the silence between your heartbeats
> hides a summons.

Do you hear it?
Name it, if you must,
or leave it forever nameless,
but why pretend it is not there?

TERMA COLLECTIVE,
The Box

4. Tell a part of your story. A good way to begin is to share the story of how you came to this gathering yourself, thereby grounding the spiritual in the personal journey. Describe your calling to start a women's spirituality group. Hearing you speak from the heart about your calling will help people to identify with parts of your story and to ponder their own. As part of this beginning, state your vision for the group in broad strokes. Before proceeding further, give them an overview of the agenda for the evening.

5. Introduce and practice council sharing. Since council sharing is such an integral part of a women's circle, we suggest that you introduce council sharing at this point and then invite them to participate in a council sharing exercise. The exercise should be something that introduces people to one another and that helps each person to clarify her own feelings and thoughts. It should not be anything that is too heavy, that requires a lot of self-disclosure, or that is very challenging to a psychologically healthy adult.

Some ideas for opening sharing exercises:

- Ask everyone to share her expectations of the meeting and her concerns about it.

- Ask everyone to choose some article of clothing or jewelry she is wearing and tell the group about its significance or meaning to her.

- Ask everyone to tell her full name and then describe the meaning of her name, her feelings about it, or any brief story about how she got the name.

6. Go over the rest of the Circle Basics. Using the explanations above as a base, and adding your own insights and anecdotes, present the basics from the chapter 3 (council sharing, listening without an agenda, rotating leadership/shared ownership, confidentiality, taking responsibility for one's own needs, self-reflection, focus on spiritual development, and commitment) to your group. Taking them one at a time, describe the concepts and their rationale. Then ask for questions or comments. Discuss them as needed until people feel clear. The point here is not deciding exactly how your group will practice each of these eight principles, but rather describing the kind of environment you, the convener(s), have in mind so that people can decide whether or not they want to take part. You can get more specific about how to adopt the basics at a future meeting.

7. Practice another round of council sharing. At this point, you will be ready for a deeper level of sharing. People are probably feeling comfortable enough now to tell a little more about themselves. You might want to choose one of the following suggestions for this deeper sharing:

- Ask each person to describe how the spirit is calling her in her life.
- Ask each person to describe the call that brought her to this meeting.
- Ask each person to describe how she feeds herself spiritually.
- Ask everyone to describe one situation, author, piece of music, or place that helps her to feel centered.

8. Lay out the options. Explain that by the next meeting everyone will need to make some choices. First, conveners will need to find out who is still interested and who is not. Ask people to let you know now or sometime before the next meeting if they plan to attend. The first meeting will usually spur people's imaginations, and they may realize they have a few friends whom they want to invite. It is a good idea to go over the "Whom to Invite" guidelines from chapter 4.

Then let people know the kinds of decisions that will be coming up in the next few meetings:

- Focus of the group (what aspect, if any, of spirituality to focus on).
- Values and principles to guide the group.

- How people feel about the Circle Basics, and how they will be used.
- Where to meet (rotate location or keep one location).
- To food or not to food. If so, how to food?
- How long to keep the group open to new members.
- A leader or pair of conveners for the first nonintroductory meeting and a theme for the meeting.

You may even want to give people a handout with these seven decision points on it so they can be thinking about them before the next meeting.

Thank people for coming, and set the next meeting date. Make it clear that people should come to that meeting only if they are interested in continuing in the group.

9. Closing. Closing with a few moments of silence allows for integration of all that has transpired in the meeting. It also signals the relinquishing of the sacred circle and the recommencement of everyday life.

Planning Guide for First Meeting

(two and a half to three hours, depending on number of attendees)

GUIDING QUESTIONS

Prepare the space.

Have you arranged to minimize interruptions?

How will you arrange the space so people can sit in a circle?

Do you want to play music? Use incense or oils?

What will you use for an altar or centerpiece?

Do you want to leave time to center and clear with another person before the guests arrive?

Collective silence and centering.

Do you want to lead some deep breathing?

What about some simple stretches?

Inspirational reading.

> Do you want to use a reading or a song to begin the meeting?

> Is it directly related to your vision for the group?

Tell a part of your story.

> What led you to decide to start a group?

> Why is it meaningful for you?

> What is your vision for the purpose of the group?

Introduce council sharing and practice.

> What question will you use to allow people to share a little about themselves and get to know one another?

> Do you plan to use a talking bowl or another talking object?

Go over the rest of the Circle Basics.

> Are you clear on the basics? Are you ready to explain them to other people? Do you have some of your own examples and experiences to use in explaining them?

Practice another round of council sharing.

> What question will you use to move the group to greater intimacy?

Lay out the options.

> Have you thought about how you would prefer the group to operate? Are there some "must haves"? Are you prepared to consider only options that will work for you? Do you want to give them a handout with options listed?

Closing.

> Do you have ideas for a next meeting time?

The Next Few Meetings

We recommend running the next few meetings with a format similar to that of the first session, for as many meetings as it takes for the group to decide who it is and what it is up to. You may have new people, if you haven't decided to close the group yet. If so, you will need to continue some sort of introductory sharing to bring them into the circle. Review the concept of council sharing and practice it.

The core work here is forming identity and intention. Some groups we interviewed have actually written mission statements or similar documents. Our group doesn't have one in writing, but the idea has strong merits. You may want to write a statement of purpose as a way of clarifying your thoughts and coming to consensus.

In addition, consider the idea of values. What values do you want the group to practice? This, too, can be a very valuable discussion. It would make a great council-sharing question as well. Differences in purpose and values always underlie group conflicts. Gaining consensus early on can eliminate the need for lots of cleanup work.

Here are some ideas for council or discussion questions at your initial meetings:

- What do you see as the purpose of this group?
- How do you see the group focusing on its purpose?
- What policies do you think the group should adopt (for example, attendance, calling to cancel, sharing responsibilities)?
- How do you see the group spending its time in the next six months?
- What is your "ideal scene" for the group? When you think of the perfect situation for the group to be engaged in, what does it look like and feel like?

These are relationships that may take on great import in your lives. It is worth the time, in our experience, to really wrestle with and be honest about these core concerns. Just think how life might have been different if you had made the effort to answer these questions before jumping into some other relationships!

Even though the primary purpose of these meetings is to decide what you want to do and how, make sure you don't turn the circle into a committee meeting. That is, how you'll decide who you are is through getting to know who you are—who shows up, what each individual brings to the mix. So having the council sharing time is critical to this getting-acquainted process.

Two Simple Rules About Logistics

Having clear agreement on a few simple questions from the start will help the group progress smoothly: when, where, how long. That old adage "the devil is in the details" is so true! Having been in many groups over the years, we have made most of the potential mistakes. In our current group, these issues have rarely been a problem because of two rules we adopted early on: **Keep it Simple, Sweetheart,** and **Share the Load.**

With twelve very busy women in our group, we learned early on that the simpler the logistics, the better. None of us needs more details to attend to in our lives. Thus we lean toward the efficient choices in logistics: one location, fourth Tuesday of each month, no food, just show up. We find that this works well, and every time we try to change it, we get flustered. Last year a few people were taking courses on our regular meeting night, and we tried to accommodate their schedules by changing the dates of the meetings. It didn't take long for chaos to follow; people started missing meetings. This year we added the specific dates of our monthly meetings to our address and phone list, and it has eliminated all that mess.

Make an effort to share the logistical work as much as possible. If one person is making most of the effort, the psychological ownership of the group is not likely to be as strong for the ones who are not investing themselves. Then there is always the martyr problem—"I do all the work and no one appreciates it!" Don't waste even a minute on that one. Share the load. Ask for help. Don't volunteer when you don't want to.

When: How often will you meet? Once a week, a month, a quarter? There is no best time; however, the more often you meet, the faster your group will bond. What is important here is deciding upon a frequency that people can commit to. Saying you are going to meet once a week and then having only three people come makes less sense than meeting once a month if most people can actually be there.

We recommend that you set your meeting dates well in advance. In Washington, people are calendar crazed. Twelve calendar-in-hand women searching for an open evening in the next month can be one of

the more frustrating experiences ever. Once you set the date, keep it.
Unless there is an earthquake or a snowstorm, get together when you
agreed. It keeps the momentum going to keep your agreements with
one another.

Where: Again, it is not important what you decide, just that you do
what you decide. You may want to rotate locations with leaders, or you
may want to choose a central spot and always meet there. The advantage
of a central location is that people always know where to go. The advantage with rotating is that everyone gets to be in one another's homes and
to share the responsibility of hostessing.

The only caveat here is to make sure that the place you meet has adequate privacy. You are creating a sanctuary—a time and place set aside
for the sacred. Few of us live alone, but it is possible to take the phone
off the hook, have the kids in bed or upstairs, and keep the passersby to
a minimum.

Food: Will you serve it or not? Will you eat a meal together before
you sit in the circle? What kind of food works for people? Some groups
we know always eat together. It is one of their signature activities. Our
group, on the other hand, in the service of simplicity, has settled on tea
and juice. That is almost the only thing we ever offer people because it
keeps preparation to a minimum.

Let It Unfold

This initial period of your group, its infancy, is all about bonding. Some
of you with voracious appetites for life may feel impatient. You want to
get to the good stuff, the soul baring. This is the only way to get there.
There is no way to successfully skip this step. Just as you need to move
slowly and consciously, stretching and waking up the body, before you
begin vigorous exercise, so you must move slowly and consciously here.
Expect some people to take longer than others to feel safe enough to
begin unfolding. You can't rip open the petals of a flower and expect it to
be a beautiful blossom. Many encounter groups in the sixties made this
mistake, and how many of them are still around? Wait and do your part
by showing up and taking small risks.

Allow a gradual beginning by choosing topics that give people plenty
of room to stick their toes in and test the water. Or do a double back flip

off the diving board, if that's their style. Aim for somewhere between cocktail party chatter and est.

In chapter 8 we have suggested a few themes for early meetings that are fairly gentle ways of beginning. These themes include spiritual fore-mothers, childhood religion, connections with the natural world, and creativity. Here are a few more of our favorite warm-up themes:

The Art of Listening

Relationships with Animals

Where Do You Call Home?

Color and Its Effects

Inspiration—What Inspires You?

Music and Spirituality

Fun—How Do You Have It?

Hand and Foot Massage Night

We are talking about trusting here—and that old-fashioned word, *faith*. You have set your intention, you have called together your people, and now all you can do is allow the universe to do its thing. Don't worry, it will. The wonderful thing is, it will likely be better than you ever even imagined.

*when I let
my defenses go
blessings come
running.*

MACRINA WIEDERKEHR

Seasons of Your Heart

6

The Power of Storytelling

*The story—from "Rumpelstiltskin" to "War and Peace"—is one
of the basic tools invented by the human mind, for the purpose
of gaining understanding. There have been great societies
that did not use the wheel, but there have been no
societies that did not tell stories.*

URSULA LE GUIN,
"Prophets and Mirrors," The Living Light

When women get together, we talk. We get down to it: Who are you? Where are you from? Where have you been? How did you get here? Who is important to you? What is important to you? Whom do you love? How do you love? Are you loved well? In short, how does life look and feel and taste and smell from your vantage point?

Our culture generally derides this womanly tendency. There are lots of jokes about gabbing, cat talk, and gossiping. However, this drive to know one another intimately, if undertaken consciously, can be a great source of learning and growth for both the teller and her audience. As listeners, we get to ponder alternate lives, feel alternate feelings, and see alternate realities. We are expanded by our curiosity, even though it is sometimes threatening to consider that ours might not be the only way, the *right* way to look at life.

Gaining Access to the Truth

Telling stories is a way of gaining access to the truth. When women start telling their stories, they begin to hear themselves echoed in the stories of others. They start to feel less weird and less isolated, and they begin trusting themselves.

Powerful, integrative, healing storytelling happens when a woman speaks solely from the perspective of her own experience. "I feel . . ." "I see . . ." "It appears to me . . ." Florida Scott-Maxwell wrote, "You need only claim the events of your life to make yourself yours. When you truly possess all you have been and done, which may take some time, you are fierce with reality." Thus, even if one is recounting a period or an event that was very painful, the telling of the story can be empowering because it acknowledges both responsibility and the life lessons afforded by the pain.

Stories Are Subjective

Powerful storytelling reflects an understanding that our realities are inherently subjective. When a woman is growing and learning, she will regularly undergo shifts in her view of the world and her place in it. Today's stories reflect the people we are today. In six months or six years, these same lives won't sound quite the same.

However, if stories are told without the knowledge of their own subjectivity, they can be far more destructive than constructive. We all know people who tell the same stories relentlessly, the ones with the same villains and the same unhappy endings. This kind of storytelling only serves to reinforce their view of themselves as victims of circumstance. It keeps them stuck in their tragedy, and it is ultimately disempowering. Research shows that depression gets worse with self-pitying attention.

How paradoxical, then, that it is only when one speaks from a consciously individual perspective that one can reveal

The universe is made of stories / not of atoms.

....

MURIEL RUKEYSER

The Speed of Darkness

the truth of universal experience. When we share *these* kinds of stories, we become teachers for each other.

We love to tell stories in our circle, and we have found them powerful medicine indeed. In chapter 8 we offer suggestions for different themes for your meetings, including questions that you can use to inspire sharing and storytelling. By way of example, we and a few of our friends will tell you a little about our journeys, using some guiding questions from the topic "Childhood Religion: The Faith of Our Fathers," in chapter 8, which focuses on each person's religious upbringing.

1. What was your religious upbringing like?

2. How did you feel about this when you were a child?

3. How does this upbringing influence the person you are today?

Sally's Story

My first religious memory was of going to church while visiting the town in Texas where I was born. My grandmother went to the Episcopal church because it was the social thing to do. My great-grandmother practiced her religion in the garden on Sunday, and on most other mornings. But I went with my cousin Betty to the Methodist Sunday school kindergarten class. In Sunday school they had Christian coloring books. I was mortified. I knew none of the names, recognized none of the pictures. I knew I was in the wrong place at the wrong time, for my parents had definitely not introduced me to traditional Christianity.

My young parents, Bill and Caroline Banks, had grown up in Arkansas and Texas and were fleeing what they saw as a provincial and narrow-minded lifestyle. Both were college educated. No Baptist hellfire and damnation for them; they were going to raise their kids as Unitarians. While visiting my grandparents in Kansas City, they took

The difference between mad people and sane people . . . is that sane people have variety when they talk-story. Mad people have only one story that they talk over and over.

MAXINE HONG KINGSTON
The Woman Warrior

me to a Unitarian church right after I was born. I was named there—Sally Love Banks, the fourth woman to have this name. The first was a Sallie Love who married a Banks. She grew up on a plantation in the Mississippi Delta near Memphis. One of my most treasured possessions is a portrait of her I recently acquired when my grandmother died. It hangs in my dining room and reminds me that I have a lineage, that I didn't just spring forth by accident and out of nowhere.

Mom and Dad moved the family to Long Island. Dad became a statistician at the United Nations, and our family with four kids under five settled into a tiny house in Levittown. This was a heavily Catholic working-class neighborhood. We were different. I hated it when people asked me where I went to church, because they invariably hadn't heard of Unitarianism. It was a strange religion to them, sounding vaguely like communism. Our Sunday school classes might take us to the Museum of Natural History or the Statue of Liberty or a local synagogue. Gertrude Banks, my paternal grandmother, was the quintessential Unitarian matriarch and one of the founders of the First Unitarian Church of Albuquerque.

I, of course, yearned for belonging even if it meant donning the parochial school outfits of my friends. Being a Unitarian in Levittown in the 1950s was a bit like being Jewish in Amarillo. One Ash Wednesday, I went for ashes with Sue, my Catholic best friend. She hadn't told me I would have to make a confession first. I suddenly found myself in a little closet, stuttering to the priest, making up some fictitious sin, getting absolved, and getting those ashes on my forehead. There, I finally looked like I belonged. When I got home, my parents couldn't hide their amusement. My dad teased me, and I was so mortified I wanted to crawl under the table.

Liberal Religious Youth, LRY for short, was the Unitarian youth group. In no way did I consider it cool. Even so, my youngest brother recently told me how the LRY had saved his sanity in a very rough time. Being superficially dutiful, though, I went along for a few years, but what I really wanted was to be a cheerleader. I even tried my hand at teaching Sunday school.

Being raised Unitarian didn't give me very much to sink my teeth into or even to rebel against. I often wonder how I would have fared growing up in a family with more traditional leanings. But what Unitarianism did offer me was respect and tolerance for other religious traditions. It also validated the notion that being on a spiritual path meant not only being open to new ideas, but also actively seeking them out.

Iris's Story

My sense of religion while growing up centered mainly around family holidays. I anticipated Hanukkah like I anticipated my birthday. I got lots of presents, and we played a record of children singing Hanukkah songs. My sister and I loved to sing along (even though we didn't really know the Hebrew words) and sarcastically imitated the Israeli narrator's English. I could never understand why he called Hanukkah a "minor holiday"—it was a big deal to us. I loved lighting the menorah and eating potato latkes. And, of course, the presents. I knew the story of the destruction of the Jewish temple, and something about Maccabees and oil that lasted eight days when they thought it would last only one. That didn't seem like a huge deal to me. What I didn't realize then, but I know now, is that Hanukkah was a big fuss only because it was competing with the commercialized holiday of Christmas.

When I was very young, Santa Claus visited us, coming down the chimney and filling stockings with gifts. My parents drove us around our neighborhood to look at all the beautiful lights decorating Christian homes. We eventually learned that we didn't get to have lights and a tree because we were Jewish and that Santa Claus was not real. Santa stopped visiting us because he was part of Christmas.

Passover was a good holiday because we got to go to Cleveland and visit our grandparents' extended family. We learned to endure the torture of sitting at the table for what seemed like an eternity, retelling the story of Moses leading the Jewish people out of slavery. The matzo ball soup and gefilte fish were highlights, as was great-uncle Phil, who'd wave his big earlobes and ask me every year if I remembered him.

My parents had moved from Ohio to northern Virginia before I was born. They chose Virginia over Maryland because they had "had enough of living in an overly Jewish neighborhood," I was told.

I liked Sunday school, which I attended from around age five. My mother came to public school at Hanukkah to make potato latkes for my

73

classmates, and I felt special. When I was six, my parents divorced. Mom would take my sister and me to temple, and Dad would pick us up and keep us for the rest of the afternoon.

Twice a week I attended religious school. I was very intimidated by Hebrew and the pressure of the bat mitzvah. My parents didn't force me when, at age eleven or so, I stated that I didn't want to go to religious school anymore. I didn't like the gruff teachers. I don't think my parents knew how hard Hebrew was for me. I didn't practice enough. Neither of my parents could read Hebrew or had had a bar or bat mitzvah cere- mony. When I was fourteen, I went back to religious school by choice. I thought I might be able to learn some answers to the questions that life was giving me. I was confirmed at age fifteen.

I resented my Judaism. It made me different from the kids I went to public school with, and as a child, fitting in is important. After I was told "get out of here, you dirty Jew" on the playground in the fourth grade, I made a practice of telling only my closest friends that I was Jewish. That's about the time I stopped going to religious school. I was a shy kid, not too athletic or popular. I didn't know any other kids in my class who were Jewish or who had divorced parents. Being Jewish was just another way that I felt like a misfit.

Because I knew I was Jewish, I wanted to follow Jewish traditions. It made me angry when my mother would sneak Tic-Tacs during Yom Kip- pur services. We were supposed to fast (which we never did), and eating in temple really embarrassed me. I also got angry when my mom and sister put up a "Hanukkah bush" (tree) in our living room one year. If we were Jewish, we were not supposed to follow the customs of Christmas. I was first angry at being Jewish and then angry that Jewish customs were not embraced in our home.

When I returned from college as an adult, I went back to the temple to reconnect with my "Jewish family." I was living with my father, but my mother, sister, and friends from childhood had moved away. Pho- tographs of me at my consecration and confirmation still hung in the same spot in our synagogue that they had when I was young. Everything had changed, it seemed, but Judaism and my temple were still there as they always had been. There for me when I needed answers, when I needed familiarity.

I became active in Jewish life in many ways, including teaching in the religious school. I taught fourth grade Jewish studies for a year and a half. I started taking Hebrew lessons when my first class of students started learning Hebrew.

After college, I was involved in the formation of a group whose goal was to form a sense of Jewish community for people in my age group. It was a success, but since I was still living in Virginia, I was still very much a minority. I moved to Washington and then Montgomery County, Maryland, searching for a community and congregation that suited me better.

I recently found a congregation that had the feel I wanted. It calls itself "the caring community." It is very warm, family oriented, and creative—all things that are important to me. Unfortunately, the membership in my age group is very low. So I started another group, this time taking a leadership role. I now feel like an important member of my temple family, and I have created what I need. I have learned to draw on my own strength and enthusiasm, sharing it with others who, like me, want to learn more about what Judaism can be in our lives.

All in all, I guess what I've gotten from my childhood experiences with Judaism is a feeling of being part of a community, the comfort of ritual, a set of moral values, and an awareness of how religion can create either separateness or connection between people.

Joyce's Story

I was born and raised in a small, homogenous community in southeastern Ohio in a working-class Catholic family of Eastern European ancestry. One of my earliest memories is kneeling beside my grandfather during Sunday mass and playing with the hat holders. Because I had a great-aunt Agnes, I always anticipated the priest calling on "Agnes . . . and all of the saints who have done Your will throughout the ages" during the Eucharistic prayers. I was proud that my aunt apparently had a special connection to God and, therefore, with getting me into heaven.

Like many children, I was taught to say my prayers each night at bedtime. Among the first prayers I learned were "Angel of God" and "Now I Lay Me Down to Sleep." I always ended my prayers by asking God to bless every family member and friend I could think of, trying not to leave anyone out. I would then kiss Jesus on the small cross at the end of my pearl rosary beads hanging from my bedpost and hope that I would not "die before I awoke."

Every spring my sister and I made a May altar in the corner of my bedroom to honor Mary, mother of Jesus. Daily we tended the vases of freshly picked lilacs and wildflowers that paid homage to Mary and filled my room with the sweetest of scents. Knowing that Mother Mary was looking down on me as I slept gave me great comfort.

As a teenager, I made it my goal to be otherwise occupied when the rest of the family went to mass on Sundays. I yearned for the space to be alone and to feel the joy and spiritual wholeness I so often felt during mass. The sounds of the choir singing "Alleluia," the scent of the incense burning during high masses, the chants of the priests who paraded down the grand aisles of our church all soothed me and helped me close out the worries and insecurities of adolescence and open my heart and soul to God's loving presence.

I guess I loved being Catholic, although I never thought of it in those terms while growing up. I knew little else. Looking back, I can see how much I loved and relied on the many religious rituals that gave rhythm to my family life. Such rituals included giving up "something" for Lent, eating fish on Fridays, taking a basket of food to the church to be blessed the day before Easter, making May altars, choosing a beautiful white lace dress for my First Holy Communion, attending mass for holy days of obligation (my favorite was All Souls Day), lighting the Advent candles, and anticipating eating the traditional Christmas Eve dinner that my mother's family had made for generations. Over the years, the celebration and honoring of these traditions helped build the foundation of my religious, cultural, and psychological identity and certainly my values. Knowing what would happen and when gave me a sense of order, predictability, and, most important, the security and comfort of feeling that I belonged.

All of this was not without conflict, of course. In my college years, when my feminist and political consciousness was emerging, I felt great discomfort and conflict between what I had learned as a Catholic girl and what I was independently coming to believe in young adulthood. The Catholic Church's positions on birth control, abortion, divorce, women's role in the church, and women's ordination caused me rage and resentment. As my disillusionment grew, I began to "church-hop" from Episcopalian to Quaker to no spiritual community at all. Only in the last five years have I fully acknowledged and embraced the Catholic spirituality with which I was raised and that is central to my identity.

Fortunately, I was not taught that Catholicism was better than any other expression of faith. I was taught that the greatest contribution one could make was to work for peace and justice and to help people in need. These teachings played an important role in my job choices and career path. I owe these lessons to my parents and to the other loving, open-minded, and deeply spiritual women and men who were my catechism teachers in high school.

In recent years, with the passing of close family and friends, I have found great comfort in the prayers and rituals from childhood. As I have reconnected with the spirituality I felt so deeply as a child and adolescent, I have found a greater capacity to live life more fully and to experience more joy. I am so thankful for the religious seeds my parents helped me plant early in life. They are again being nourished to grow and blossom.

Meredith's Story

You ask what was it like growing up as a Baptist? For me it started when I first entered St. Stephen's Baptist Church, where the sign in front of the building proudly proclaims that you are in the "Friendly Church on the Corner." When you ask what has influenced my view of religion and the impact it has had on my life, the answer is probably rooted in the people and experiences in that church. I don't remember a time when I didn't enter those doors. Getting ready for Sunday school always started Saturday night, with our baths and getting our hair done. Our Sunday clothes were always laid out by my mother. Going to Sunday school was the formal part of my education and relationship with God and church. My mother, who was and is a revered Sunday school teacher, always made God and Jesus a part of our daily lives, through constant reference, prayer, and conversation. It was as if he was an unseen relative who resided within our home. God seemed very accessible. Sunday school was the time and place where we came together as families to rejoice, praise, testify, and observe others in the act of worship. Sunday school was where I learned about Samson, David and Goliath, Peter, and Paul. I also learned that I was a part of a community.

Sunday school was the first place I had the chance to perform, by reciting my Easter or Christmas piece. I vividly recall those days and nights spent practicing to ensure that my brother and I could give flawless presentations. After all, who wanted to stand before that sea of encouraging and loving eyes and forget lines? Church was where adults, other than your family, sought you out to compliment you on your hair ribbons or on how well you had read that verse or sung that song. It was the place where people spoke of God's love and used phrases like "God bless you," "for heaven's sake," and "Lord have mercy" as a part of every conversation.

Sunday school was where singing and song were a major part of every service, and those years of Sundays etched dozens of gospel hymns and spirituals into my head and heart so that today, decades later, they flow effortlessly from my lips. These songs were the same ones that I sang to each of my children as I rocked them to sleep as infants and still sing each night when they have trouble falling asleep. These songs were sung to me by my mother and sung to eulogize my father. These are the songs that I still long to hear, because they remind me that "I Come to the Garden Alone," that there is an "Old Ship of Zion," and that I continuously ask my "Precious Lord" to "Take My Hand." They call me to "Be Thankful."

Sunday school was also the place where I learned to emulate others, and my role model was Phyllis Mason, the Sunday school secretary. She counted the offering, recorded the attendance, and reported this and other church announcements each Sunday. She had everything I wanted when I was nine or ten years old—style, sophistication, and grace. In today's vernacular, "Phyllis had it goin' on." She made you love to hear those announcements. I grew up wanting that job, and when I was fifteen I finally got it. Years later, I still smile with delight when others recall my stint as the Sunday school recording secretary, a melodic title that rings in my ears. This was the first time I remember having status, position, and responsibility in my church.

While Sunday school was a place of joyfulness, the eleven o'clock service was quite different. It seemed most formidable, always more serious and a little scary for me as a child. I used to be curious, a little in awe, and definitely aware that something very different was going on in "church." In our sanctuary, the elder men, the deacons, would assemble before the altar and begin to chant and sing in tones that seemed like moaning. The first time I heard this, I couldn't imagine what these men were doing down on their knees with their heads bowed and eyes closed as they moaned out songs I had never heard. The moans sounded like pain in the innermost chambers of their being. But the moans gave over to prayer, which always started with thanks "for waking us up this morning" and "for bringing us to this house of the Lord." This was probably the first time I had ever considered that waking up might not be a foregone and predictable event, even though it had been repeated thousands of mornings already in my short life.

As the deacons ended, there was even a stronger voice of reassurance that God would be with us today and for the rest of our life to come. This voice would always signal the start of church, and the ministers would enter and the choir procession begin. Some folks, like my mother and father, had seats where they always sat, and regardless of whether or not they were there, no one else sat in those seats. My parents always sat to the right of the center aisle, fourth row from the front. It was if there was an invisible sign that read "Reserved Only for the Springs Family."

The order of service was usually the same. There always seemed to be a lot of talking. The talking would be broken up by people who would "catch the spirit." It appeared that some force seemed to take over the person, who would often holler, shout, cry, and laugh at the same time. From my small vantage point, it was a little scary. By the time I was seven or eight, I hoped that I would never catch that spirit, because it appeared to completely take over the person. I was convinced I didn't want that. That feeling persisted for many years, and when I was in my thirties I even came to question whether or not I was truly saved since I "hadn't caught the spirit" or had not had an earth-shaking conversion that signaled God's presence in my life.

And so for many years I distanced myself from the influence of my early relationship with God and the church. In my twenties I became too busy and too preoccupied with my life to spend any time with God. Always in the nagging recesses of my mind, heart, and soul was a voice questioning me. During that period, while visiting my parents, I would hope against hope that my mother wouldn't bring up God's name. But of course, he resided there, and his presence was still overwhelming.

As I moved into my thirties, a series of life events challenged me to return to that reassurance that I had always found in God and my church. In those moments of great loss when I seemingly had nowhere else to turn, God's grace engulfed me and pulled me through. I was back home, back to the familiar, back to the predictability of so many things like the cadence of the Baptist preacher or the ritual of standing and sitting during services. I came to realize that, for me, not only did it made sense, but without it *nothing* made sense.

No matter where I have moved, worked, or lived, St. Stephen's still holds me. I got married there. I took each of my children there to have them dedicated to the church as infants. And, most recently, I buried my father there. Through each and every event, the people of that community have held me. They still claim me as their own. They provide gracious and loving prayer and support. They treat me as the collective "crown jewel," the woman who left their midst only to make good and make them proud. Their loving witness is a constant call to me to remember that to whom much is given, much is asked, and it is my blessing to be one to whom much has been given.

Robin's Story

This is an important story for me, one that has shaped my life as much as, if not more than, any other. It keeps changing as I change. In telling it again and again I see myself, Spirit, and my life journey differently each time.

I was born into a Southern Baptist family, steeped in the Bible, stewed in church. Church was the dominant religious influence of my life, and I can easily say I spent my first twenty years trying to "get" fundamentalism and the last twenty trying, sometimes desperately, to get over it.

The church of my childhood was monolithic. When I think of it, I immediately associate with my grandmother's church in Kentucky. This was the church my father was raised in, and in many ways it served as the religious incubator for all his children while he struggled to find some resolution to his own unvoiced and festering spiritual quandaries.

Visits to my grandmother several times a year meant an intense immersion in a fundamentalism that we, by contrast, merely skimmed the

surface of in our daily lives in suburban Washington, D.C. At Grandmother's there were Sunday school and worship service, which consumed the entire Sunday morning. Preparations began early for all the
family members. Hair was brushed and braided, faces were washed, and
mouths fed. As the scheduled departure time approached, tensions
mounted, for children always develop resistance any time adults need to
present their families as well groomed, well behaved, and on time. (I remember one time laughing hysterically after realizing that my little sister, Becky, had managed to attend church without any underpants on
under her dress! The thought of it was deliciously disgraceful.)

The unerring routine of the worship service is ingrained in my
memory. Over thirty-five years later I can still hear the sharp tone of
the preacher's voice, the stale smell of the large austere sanctuary, and
the eternal boredom of waiting for the final prayer. All of this was
punctuated only by the relief of occasional hymns. I liked to follow
along in the hymnbook and sing really loudly. Then it was home to a
huge dinner of superb Southern cooking and time to play until supper.
After supper we were back to church for another meeting. During the
week we attended Training Union on Wednesday nights, and if we happened to be visiting during the summer, all the children were enrolled
in daily Vacation Bible School.

In addition to the sensate details, I have powerful emotional memories as well of Grandmother's church. I don't think people were having
much fun. And even though there were hymns and sermons and readings
about joyfulness, I could see none of it actually happening. Rather, it appeared to me, the adults had a dutiful, disciplined, even rigorous attitude toward the whole affair. Church wasn't awful, just numbingly dull
and heavy.

The content, the message, and the punch line of all this were not lost
on me. What I learned was that there were lots of rules to follow if you
want to go to heaven—the Ten Commandments, of course, but they
were just the beginning. Add to them obedience, chastity, modesty, and
honesty. I was taught that I was born a sinner, naturally inclined to evil.
That Jesus saves people from themselves. I felt like a failure at the
outset. There was no way that I could be good enough to be a Christian,
but I tried to keep up a convincing front and hoped my shortcomings
wouldn't be too obvious.

It was all very clear, straightforward, and rational. If you do these things, you are in. If you do these things, you are out—and I mean really out. Hell was described frequently, sparing no sensual or psychological detail. As for God himself, he appeared to me to be harsh, judging, and punishing. There was no mystery. The church's TRUTH was the only TRUTH. Take it or take it. There was no magic. It was as flat, as imperative, as unyielding, and as blunt as a concrete slab.

My intuition, even as a child, led me to wonder about much of this. For one thing, I could never figure out why all those little kids living in China were going to have to go to hell when they didn't even have a church to go to. Likewise, why would God create humans in the first place if they were so bad, so unworthy, so sinful from the start? I never heard anyone question the church or the veracity of each and every word of the Bible. So I decided to keep my questions to myself.

By the time I was ten years old, I was becoming aware of the evidence all around me that men were higher in the religious hierarchy than women. Women were to obey men, I was taught. Men ran the show at church, at work, and at home. They knew better. They were closer to God. Case closed. These are lessons I am still unlearning. It took two unhappy marriages, many overly deferential relationships with overbearing bosses, and years of therapy before I stopped handing the authority for my life over to men and then resenting them for taking it.

During adolescence I abandoned my always inadequate attempts to stay on God's good side. I had a stormy, rebellious, self-destructive few years that included an abortion, running away from home for nearly a year, and having a son when I was barely sixteen years old. According to the rules of the church, I had blown it completely. When I was twenty, I became a "born-again" Christian and did my best to catch the train to salvation. But after a diligent few years of daily Bible reading, a prayer group, and regular church attendance, I finally had to admit that I just didn't get it. I heard the words, I said the words. I did not feel the words.

Since then I have explored Eastern mysticism, yoga and yogic philosophy, Jungian psychology, and many other realms of spirituality. I even attended Harvard Divinity School but decided it was overly intellectual and too patriarchal for me. Now I am most at home with the gentle and self-affirming principles of Kripalu yoga. I teach yoga and dance and find that learning to treat my body as a sacred temple has been essential in healing and in finding a relationship with Spirit that is loving and empowering. In my "religion" not only does God have a feminine face, she also encourages fun, joy, magic, creativity, freedom, and mystery.

As I look back I see that my lifelong spiritual search has been, at least in part, born out of a need to make peace with the intense, judging, disturbing presence of the God I was introduced to as a child. In that sense, I feel thankful that, though mostly negative, my childhood religion made such a strong impression on me that I have spent much of my life energy addressing the questions and issues it raised.

Had I been brought up in a family where religion was treated more casually, perhaps I never would have been interested in feminism or spirituality or gotten involved in women's groups or written this book (which, by the way, has been one of the most joyful experiences of my life). Thus, though painful and confusing, my religious upbringing has profoundly shaped my life, always leading me to search for my own answers to life's questions.

Carol's Story

I was raised a Catholic, and I went to the first two years of college at a Catholic girls' college. Have you heard the phrase "recovering Catholic"? Well, I would more accurately call myself a "rebellious Catholic."

When I was a child, faith was the most precious thing I had—my religious practices and my daily devotion to Jesus, the Christ. I took everything absolutely seriously—my first Holy Communion, catechism, and confirmation. I even think I was aware of my baptism, and I was only a preschool child. I loved the stations of the cross. I thought they were deep and tragically meaningful. I knew that people felt an intense adoration for the Blessed Mother, but that didn't really distract me from my focus on the relationship I had with Jesus. I felt him and trusted him with all my heart. I even believed that the sins I did commit would automatically be okay with him because of how much I loved him. I didn't sin very often, though. As a child I used to confess all the sins I thought about. Those were the only ones I had to tell at confession. The thought sins always had to do with sex.

I eventually became a novice for a day. Really! I actually went to the Felician Order. The day I went to be fitted for my habit (interesting

term) I had to kneel at the altar of the chapel and make my final decision. I had a talk with Jesus that day, and he told me that he had work for
me to do on the outside and that my talents would not be best developed
in the convent. I left the altar and told my best friend, the nun, with
whom, incidentally, I was in love, that I had changed my mind. For a
while I felt terrible, like I would be cursed. But I got over it.

It was after I transferred from the Catholic college to the state university that the rebellious person was born. For the next several years I
did everything I wasn't supposed to do. I studied transcendental meditation and an array of Eastern philosophies and religions. I was even initiated as a Sufi. I made it through that four years and became a Muslim for
the next ten. I loved the rituals and praying five times a day.

During the whole time I was a Muslim, however, I kept my devotion
to Jesus. I even learned a Muslim prayer, *La Il Allah-Il-Allah,Wa Ini Isa Ruh
Allah*, which (in my translation) means, "There is one God and Jesus is
the soul of God" (or "breath of God"). It was late in 1983 that I was
praying the afternoon *salat* when I heard a voice from within me ask,
"Do you know what the word *Islam* means?" I answered to myself, yes, it
means desire for light. The voice inside me replied, "I am the Light."

I returned to Christianity after that and joined a nondenominational
church. During the time when I began to develop my Christian relationship with Jesus, I reevaluated my religious affiliations. I decided that
Catholicism was very sacred and the rituals were holy and devout. I saw
many universal truths expressed in its practices, but I found that for me
it was not entirely relevant.

I later joined an African American Baptist Church, where I feel right
at home. I am now in the choir at my home church, and many of its
practices are inclusive of Catholic and Episcopal rites. The bottom line is
that most of the people in the church look, sound, and act like relatives
of mine. I think of all the various religions I have practiced, the various
influences that helped me to self-actualize. It has been a winding road,
but it has been well worth every turn.

Becky's Story (Robin's Sister)

I was brought up with conservative Christian values where biblical
ethics like honesty and doing unto others as you would have them do

unto you were not only taught but modeled. Although my parents later stopped going to church and changed their views on Christianity, I was given a foundation that life had absolutes—a set of standards for determining right and wrong and a God (Jesus Christ) who transcended the goings-on of humans but was also interested in interacting with them.

In junior high school I began attending a church youth program with a friend. I distinctly remember that first Friday night meeting. The speaker explained that "all had sinned and fallen short of the glory of God." He further explained that God loved me thoroughly and desired a relationship with me, and that he provided a way of reconciliation through his perfect son, Jesus Christ. He (the speaker) said that I could know beyond the shadow of a doubt that my relationship with God and my entrance into heaven were secured by putting my faith and trust in Jesus Christ.

Despite all my years of churchgoing as a child, I had never heard this message so clearly, and when the youth pastor invited those who wanted to express their faith in Jesus to raise their hands, I did so. That was the first step in my journey of faith. Over the next several years I attended an evangelical Bible church, where I was given verse-by-verse instruction from what I still believe to be God's word. I found, and still find, the principles I learned to be trustworthy for practical decision making in everything from financial matters to marriage and child rearing.

Despite the fact that I saw clearly that God's favor could not be earned by my actions, my own personality and people-pleasing tendencies led to my desire to perform for others, rather than trying to please God. And so these early years were filled with a combination of sincere and zealous enthusiasm as well as a large measure of righteous condemnation of myself and others.

I look back with gladness that I was strongly grounded in God's principles. My passion for living them out protected me from many destructive pitfalls of adolescence. And I am thankful that my church was a place not only where was I challenged and accepted, but also where my leadership skills and musical abilities could flourish. I felt like I belonged and that the church gave me a sense of bearing. I grew in my understanding of spiritual issues and in my confidence as a person.

But now I look back with sadness that my strong feelings about Christianity made me uncomfortable with anything outside the very narrow margins that I had drawn for what was "okay." And even though I knew the scriptures spoke of God's abiding love for me, I was still inwardly and outwardly trying to measure up. I had a code of regulations about nearly everything—what to eat, how to celebrate certain holidays, what kind of music was permissible. It was mentally and emotionally exhausting, and I felt guilty most of the time.

My dad said to me once, "You Christians say that God makes you free, but from what I can see, I'm freer than you because I'm not bound up by all those laws." What he said haunted me. He knew I was walking around with a long list of unwritten rules in my head. I knew in my heart that my dad spoke the truth and that this wasn't the freedom Christ intended.

When my eighteen-month-old daughter was diagnosed with cancer, all pretenses of faith were stripped away. All the energy to keep up the religious trappings suddenly dissolved. My list of rules suddenly seemed inconsequential. My ability to please God with performance and attitude was gone. I couldn't even pray. How could the child of a God-fearing and Bible-believing person be stricken with a mortal illness? This didn't fit my paradigm.

I knew that it wasn't about my praying enough for my child or believing hard enough for her to get well or taking comfort in scriptural promises (all the things I would have projected onto someone else in similar circumstances). It wasn't even about whether God would heal her or let her die. It was about God being sufficient to sustain me. It was only when I was too tired and weak to try to please God that I began to realize his intense and unconditional love for me. It was in my inability to prove myself to him that he proved himself to me. This shift changed my life.

I still believe in Jesus Christ and I feel thankful that I've had a little more of a glimpse of his amazing grace. His principles are still practical for real life, and his Holy Spirit is alive within me. But I no longer have tidy little laws for every occasion. I can see that all efforts to understand God (hah!) and control my life by my internal code of conduct were really efforts to feel safe. Yet the more I've really given control over my life to him, the safer I feel.

Authors' note: Becky's daughter, Taylor, survived chemotherapy and major surgery. She is now almost four years old and looks vibrant and healthy in every way. Though a small bit of tumor is still lodged in her spine, the cancer is not growing, and her chances for a full recovery are good.

Nancy's Story

In retrospect, all my life has been searching for God and desiring to serve God.

In my earliest consciousness, my father and God were inseparable. My father was, in his words, "married" to his work as a minister. He had decided as a teenager to serve the "world's greatest need," which he gradually realized to be a spiritual need. His intense sense of religious mission consumed him and our family.

My father had mystical visions. He learned to keep quiet about them, but they seem to have given him an extraordinary sense of certainty. As a little girl, when I learned about Moses, Jesus, and all the other strong, visionary leaders up there with God, I thought they must be just like my father. As far as I could see, my mother agreed. All three of us believed my father was always right.

Our bedtime ritual was reading the Bible, talking and asking questions, and then saying the Lord's Prayer together. It was a sweet, warm-feeling time. I learned that God had two important qualities, love and truth, each necessary to the other. There were seven layers of heaven and of hell. Hell was not exactly a punishment. A person who lied and cheated, for example, would be happiest in a world where everyone was dishonest. So liars and cheaters were sent to one of the levels of hell with other people like them. I wanted to become one of God's highest angels, and I told my parents my dreams about God.

When my rabbit died, I had questions about death. I was told that the angels arranged for a person to be in a place very similar to the one she had left so that she would not have a sudden shock. Taking this to heart, I often wondered if I were still alive. "Maybe I just died and don't know it yet!" Death was unreal, but so was life. Much later, in my twenties, I began to push through the soothing, deadening denial and to face my fear of death. The energy of fear transformed into longing to be alive and joy that I am alive.

Our church was the Church of the New Jerusalem, a Protestant denomination based on the writings of Emanuel Swedenborg. Swedenborg was a scientist in the seventeenth century who at the age of fifty began to have visions. Angels took him on tours of heaven and hell and revealed the mysteries of God's word. Swedenborg wrote his Arcana Celestia (secrets of heaven) in Latin, and even in translation his writings were very dense. You had to be a serious scholar to belong to this church.

My father taught that "this life is a school and training ground for the next life." If God loves you, he gives you really hard lessons! True to this idea, my parents suffered a lot. They were always tired and under stress. We were poor and in debt. My mother had grand mal epileptic seizures, and my father had severe migraine headaches. From the time I was very little, when my mother was having frequent seizures, I would be taken away for a week or a month to stay with my grandparents.

When I was five years old my father took a principled stand that divided his congregation. They resolved the conflict by throwing him out. Ours was a very small denomination, and there was no other church for my father.

Around the same time, my mother's epilepsy was tamed by medication. She went to "normal school" to fulfill her dream of becoming a teacher, and my father took factory jobs. We rented rooms in other people's homes, and because these living situations were not tolerable for long, we moved every few months to a new town and a new school district. Finally, I was sent to live with my grandparents for a year because my parents "couldn't give me a normal home." When my mother graduated, we moved from Massachusetts to rural Kansas, where my father again became the minister of a church and my mother taught kindergarten.

Here in the nineties we notice that God and all the important mythical figures of Protestant Christianity are all male. Back then that fact was as invisible as the air we breathe. My family was a reflection of this celestial pattern. In my family the man was the grown-up, the more important person, the one with the mission—the one who spoke passionately on Sunday mornings while everyone listened. My poor mother fought desperately to be included in the ministry (to which her man was "married"), but she "would take too long to train." My parents were feminists in theory, but the tangible message was that girls don't have it in them to be as smart, as good, as right, and as powerful as boys. I listened mutely for hours as my father talked religion, but as a girl, I was not expected to have a voice. Telling this story is part of recovering my voice.

Until I was twelve or so, I believed totally. I believed that whatever I earnestly prayed for would happen. Based on my father's beliefs about who were the good guys and who were the bad guys in national politics, I even influenced presidential elections; the Eisenhower-Nixon victory was my responsibility.

Another kind of spiritual experience happened one day on my way home from school. I was walking along in my usual state of internal pre-occupation when I looked up and was suddenly dazzled awake by sunlight on a young tree. In my current language I would say it was an epiphany or that I was fully present in the here and now, one with the tree and the sunlight. At the time I had no language for it. The experience was forgotten—to be remembered and recognized only much later.

The sojourn of my weird family and my weird self in Kansas lasted four years and came to an abrupt and painful end. A nurse violated medical confidentiality, and the school board of our tiny town learned the terrible secret of my mother's epilepsy. There was great struggle and hysteria on both sides. On the one hand, people were understandably trying to protect their children from a truly dangerous and frightening experience—the adult in charge falling down shaking and drooling and turning blue, which had happened to me many times in my early life! However, thanks to her medication, my mother was as safe a teacher as anyone else; there was no danger. In the end, they fired her. The school board president was a member of our church, and soon my father also lost his job. I feel for them now. How unfair this was! But their torment and worldly failure were part of my deciding there must be some mistakes in my parents' view of the world. Like many adolescents, I vowed that I would be different and, somehow, better.

My family arrived at my mother's parents' house broke and homeless, with all our belongings in a rented truck. My father did not seem worried. He said, "The Lord will provide. Consider the lilies of the field." My grandparents, supporting us on their slim Social Security income, came to hate my father for this arrogant attitude. (My cousin says, "He came for two weeks and stayed two years, and nobody said a word about it!") My father eventually went to live with his brother.

My father was a lily of the field for the rest of his life. He never worked again. I feel he was broken by the loss of that church and of his life's work. From that point on, he started several wonderful projects but never completed them. My mother, who was able to resume her teaching, gradually became the stronger one.

Meanwhile, at thirteen, I visited a Baptist church that my grandmother occasionally attended. I liked the simplicity of the message. Swedenborg was too complicated, I decided. If God really wanted to communicate with human beings, he would not bury his message in the labyrinth of Swedenborg's writings. I did my very best to be saved. In the next year, I even carried a Bible to school. I was excruciatingly inauthentic. Finally, my mother and I moved to rejoin my father in yet another town. I remember thinking, "Nobody knows me here, so I don't have to be who I used to be." I dropped my by-then-unbearable fundamentalism.

The next significant change happened when I was in college. Sexuality was causing great internal conflict. To be good was to be virginal, even though I had worn this down to a technicality. My boyfriend distracted me from my guilt by feeling even more guilty about corrupting an innocent girl! Even masturbation was sinful, although I do not remember being taught this. How could a good and wise God create us as sexual beings and then make sexual feelings bad?

I finally ended the conflict by throwing out everything other people had told me to believe. I felt great relief! I knew with my own heart and mind that certain things—for example, love and truth seeking—were good and that human beings had some capacity for this goodness. Bad, then, was anything that harmed these capacities. I could stand firmly on this ground and build from there.

The religion of my childhood influences me today in that I am still and always a religious person, concerned with the spiritual quality of life. I like that Jesus said, "The Kingdom of God is within you." Taking Swedenborg's teachings as metaphors rather than literal truth, I find a lot of wisdom in them. Like Swedenborg, I believe that we are punished and rewarded not for our deeds but by our deeds, by the kind of internal world we create. Heaven and hell are real-enough here-and-now possibilities for each of us.

In reaction to my upbringing, I am wary of beliefs. I see that people are capable of believing incredibly stupid and harmful things! There are spectacular examples in the newspapers. I try beliefs on like clothing. If they are useful, if they have a good effect, I keep them around in my mental closet. I am content to be humbly agnostic about the ultimate nature of the universe. On the other hand, I claim for myself all the experiences of love and joy and oneness that people call "God." I can even appeal for help from beyond-who-I-know-myself-to-be. In other words, lack of "belief" does not bar me from experiencing heaven. As a psychotherapist, I have great appreciation for the spiritual resources of others regardless of their different belief systems.

I have found a spiritual community in the Ethical Society, a religious community that spells God with two *o*s. My husband, Don, was a businessman when I married him, and we joke that I turned him into a minister, because now he is a "Leader," a clergyman in the Ethical Society. So here I am, like my mother, a "minister's wife"! However, I, too, have a sense of mission. I hope to learn and to teach about a supreme way of being rather than a supreme being. And I, too, sometimes speak passionately on Sunday mornings.

. . . .

Telling our stories is one way we become more aware of just what "the river" of our lives is. Listening to ourselves speak, without interruption, correction, or even flattering comments, we may truly hear, perhaps for the first time, some new meaning in a once painful, confusing situation. We may, quite suddenly, see how this event or relationship we are in the midst of describing relates to many others in our past. We may receive a flash of insight, a lesson long unlearned, a glimpse of understanding. And, as the quiet, focused compassion for us pervades the room, perhaps our own hearts open, even slightly, toward ourselves.

One of the problems women have today is that they are not willing to find the river in their own life and surrender to its current. They're not willing to spend time, because they feel they are being selfish. They grow up trying to please other people and they rarely ask themselves, Who am I? . . . They live in terms of pleasing rather than in terms of being who they are.

MARION WOODMAN

quoted in

The Feminine Face of God

91

7

Reclaiming Ritual

*The purpose of ritual is to wake up the old mind, to put it to
work. The old ones inside us, the collective unconscious, the
many lives, the different eternal parts, the senses and the
parts of the brain that have been ignored. Those parts
do not speak English. They do not care about television.
But they do understand candlelight and colors.
They do understand nature.*

Z BUDAPEST,
in Drawing Down the Moon

We sit facing each other, having
caught up on the latest juicy details of our lives, our families' and
friends' lives. Lighting an ivory-colored candle seated in a sea green
glass, we look into each other's eyes just briefly. We hold hands, left
right, right left, encircling the candle, which has by now begun to emit a
soothing aroma. Our eyes close. We drop into another place. Outside
noises fade, urgent errands recede. Stepping over the threshold of sacred
space, held in place for a few minutes of crystal silence.

We state our intention to serve as conduits of Spirit and to convey
the message of this book clearly. We ask for assistance and guidance,

inviting our ego-bound small selves to step aside. The interplay of will and surrender, surrender and will commences. We thank Spirit for the opportunity to do meaningful work. Silence again. Grinning, we open our eyes. The way opens. "So, where should we start today?"

And so, with such a ritual, we began each book meeting as we learned to work and create and write in a whole new way. Invariably, this small ritual allowed us to move forward with our work of coauthoring this book. Resistance melted and confusion cleared.

What Is Ritual?

The purpose of ritual is to change the mind of the human being. It's sacred drama in which you are the audience as well as the participant, and the purpose of it is to activate parts of the mind that are not activated by everyday activity.

SHARON DEVLIN,
in Drawing Down the Moon

Our purpose in writing this chapter is to encourage each of you, if you haven't already done so, to reclaim ritual as your own. What do we mean by ritual? **Ritual is the act of consciously opening ourselves to the presence of Spirit**. This is an intentionally broad definition, because, we contend, most of us have learned to understand ritual far too narrowly to serve us fully. For many of us, even the word *ritual* connotes something stale, done by rote, a lifeless routine. Throughout the book we use the words *ceremony* and *ritual* interchangeably.

If we are to reclaim our culture, we cannot afford narrow definitions.

....

STARHAWK

The Spiral Dance

Traditionally, ritual has included everything from simple prayer to labyrinthine liturgy. By our definition, planting a garden, preparing a meal, or making love can all be ceremony, depending on the consciousness in which it is done.

Timothy Leary said, "Ritual is to the internal sciences what experiment is to the external sciences." This is a wonderful description because it captures the experimental and creative nature of ritual. Not only can you do it yourself, you can do it differently every time.

Ceremony can be ours to play with rather than remaining remote and out of reach. We can approach it in different ways, use different tools, and experiment with different settings and see what happens. We can borrow from diverse traditions, throw in a little of our own imagination, and cook up a ceremonial concoction that fits just the occasion we have in front of us. And it can be lots of fun. We discuss all manner of ritual in this chapter, the silly and the serious, the scripted and the spontaneous. If rituals are undertaken with positive intent and are conducted mindfully, learning and growth will occur.

Stolen Ceremony

For most of us, ritual has been something prescribed by someone else. Webster's dictionary defines ritual as "In religious devotion or service, the practice of a certain set of formulas." Formulas—how formal! However, the word *ritual* actually is derived from the Sanskrit word *rtu,* which means any act of magic toward a purpose. Interestingly, *ritual* is related to the word for menses, and some scholars think that the earliest rituals ever developed were connected to women's monthly bleeding.

Ritual was taken out of our hands so long ago that we sometimes forget that somebody somewhere a long time ago made it all up. Traditional ceremonies performed by ordained clergy are no better or worse, no more or less spiritual, than the ritual you made up to bury your cat when you were ten years old.

Ritual was slowly and surely confiscated from women and put in the hands of priests, rabbis, and other anointed ones, as if *they* alone could reach the divine. And until a few years ago, *they* were all men. Under the rules of patriarchal religion, women who wanted to have a more direct connection to the divine could not join the clergy. They still can't in the Catholic Church or Orthodox Judaism.

A striking example of this confiscation is the way that many religions deal with menstruation and childbirth. In orthodox Judaism and Islam, not only are women not allowed to initiate and conduct certain sacred rituals, they are not even allowed to participate in ritual if they are

There are many, many gates to the sacred and they are as wide as we need them to be.

....

SHERRY RUTH ANDERSON
AND PATRICIA HOPKINS
The Feminine Face of God

95

menstruating. Likewise, childbirth is treated with ritual isolation and segregation. In these ways, and many others, our bodies and their natural functions have been used as an excuse to sever us from sacred ritual.

One of America's most astute social commentators, Linda Weltner, the *Boston Globe* columnist, has written more than one piece about women's spirituality and ritual. She described a croning ceremony to celebrate the coming into wisdom of women in her group, which meets at the Unitarian Universalist church she attends. In another piece she tells of the group's efforts to create its first full moon ritual. "We all felt uneasy, to some degree," she writes, "with the idea that we could create rituals we'd only read about. It's hard to believe you can be graceful or effective in carrying out procedures that seem strange or new." Weltner is right. It is hard to believe—hard to believe that one could have the audacity to get away with making something up and calling it a ritual. Hard, also, to believe that it could actually help or inspire or heal.

But there is more than mere inexperience underlying this uneasiness. There is also fear. Traumatic memories are lodged in our cells. The "Burning Times" are there, when our ancestors were accused of witchcraft and were hounded, persecuted, tortured, and killed. The numbers may be in question, but there is little doubt that the persecution of wise women, under the auspices of the organized church, continued from the Middle Ages well into the eighteenth century in our own country. One of Sally's ancestors, Goody Parsons, was tried for witchcraft in the Salem trials.

As we were writing this book, Hillary Rodham Clinton was savaged for her spiritual explorations with Jean Houston and Mary Catherine Bateson. Signs at the 1996 Republican National Convention referred to "Hillary the Witch." Her life may not have been threatened, but it was harsh treatment indeed for simply experimenting with new ways to gain access to Spirit's guidance.

So when we create ritual, we are doing it with the understanding, perhaps not even conscious, that our foremothers have been severely punished for such activity. Don't be surprised if in your explorations you feel the uneasiness of which Weltner speaks. You may also feel silly, embarrassed, pretentious, self-conscious, and even scared. It takes courage to reclaim ritual.

*Rituals are a good
signal to your
unconscious that it is
time to kick in.*

ANNE LAMOTT

Bird by Bird

Ritual in Everyday Life

*Rituals create moments where living becomes art. Poets, writers,
painters and musicians aspire to heightened moments of
awareness, times when they feel they have something
unique and inspiring to give the world. . . .We all
have this instinct to create beauty, distinction,
and meaning in our lives. . . .*

ALEXANDRA STODDARD,
Living a Beautiful Life

We are ritualistic beings. Our urge to ritualize, to create ceremony, can be suppressed but not suffocated. It's in our DNA. We hunger for it, and we do it even when we don't realize that it is what we are doing. Rituals and ceremony probably play a role in your life even if you aren't aware of them.

What are the simple rituals that help weave the fabric of your life together? Do you have a bed-making ritual with your partner? Do you always sit in the same place when you write letters or offer prayers or play with your cat? What about kitchen and garden rituals? Is the bathtub a ritual site for you? Do you always kiss your partner good-night? Do you hug your children when they leave? Do you visit the grave of a loved one? Do you enact certain practices around holidays? Take a few moments and trace the minor ceremonies of your day.

Christmas in Sally's home is a wonderful example of rituals connected to family traditions in ways that provide comfort, meaning, and continuity. Sally and her husband always hang the same two sets of sixty-year-old lights on the tree. They always have dinner at home on Christmas Eve—cheese fondue for the last ten years—followed by carol singing with books that have been taped and restapled many times. And she and her husband even have the same ritualistic arguments over who is going to wash the hardened cheese out of the fondue pots, and couldn't she just add one more string of newer lights to augment his parents' set?

*Ritual is the way we
carry the presence of
the sacred. Ritual is
the spark that must
not go out.*

. . . .

CHRISTINA BALDWIN

Life's Companion

97

Robin has a friend whose mother always puts on her wedding dress to make breakfast on her wedding anniversary. It doesn't fit her anymore, and so half her torso is hanging out the unzipped back, but it is a fun, lighthearted way to pay homage to her marriage.

Yes, you might say, I recognize this kind of stuff, even in my life. But what makes these things different from just plain old habits? One criteria for distinguishing ritual from habits is that ritual is the conscious and intentional reach beyond the everyday realm and into the sacred. Ritual connects us to sources of power outside ourselves that are much greater than we alone can muster. Paradoxically, a simple ritual, to an onlooker, may appear to be mundane behavior.

Take, for instance, bathing. A bath can be undertaken merely to clean our bodies, or it can be far more. Take the phone off the hook. Tell the kids the bathroom is off-limits for an hour. Light a candle and put on some soothing music. When you lower yourself into a lavender-scented bath, some part of you knows that taking a bath softens and centers, and using lavender oil aids the relaxation and heightens creativity. The intention is plainly there as you, in effect, are saying, "I need help relaxing, so I'm going to entrust this body into the capable hands of the water and essential oil spirits." It's a whole new twist to the old commercial "Calgon, take me away!" As D. M. Levin says in *The Body's Recollection of Being,*

*Rituals are formulas
by which harmony
is restored.*

....

TERRY TEMPEST WILLIAMS
Pieces of White Shell

Through ritual . . . the living body is completely reshaped. We
are touched and moved in every cell and fiber. . . . And our various
organs and sensoria, the "gates" and "pathways" of awareness, are
deeply relaxed or widely opened, so that we can begin to experience
the healing presence of that which, since time immemorial, religious
traditions have called . . . the "holy," the "sacred," and the "divine."

Simple rituals may be repeated often, and part of their power lies in this repetition, but some ceremony is spontaneous. It just naturally arises out of a particular circumstance. There are mornings like today when the sun breaking through the clouds streaks the dawn sky with such glory that one is moved to offer a prayer of praise and thanksgiving. These spontaneous rituals have a sweet kind of power. They are life-affirming reminders of the human capacity to be surprised and delighted by the unexpected.

Why We Do Rituals

*As human beings, we live just this side of an invisible membrane
separating our day-to-day consciousness from the miracle
of creation. Ceremony, by its very makeup and by the
language it speaks, has the power to sidestep our
rational minds and to penetrate this membrane,
allowing reentry into the Mystery.*

TERMA COLLECTIVE,
The Box

Ceremony helps us connect with our spiritual nature. Grace happens serendipitously, when we least expect it. There comes a moment when we realize we are in union with something much greater than ourselves. Ceremony is a way of asking grace to enter. We consciously invite Spirit to be with us and to grant us an awareness of its presence. As we cross the threshold into ceremony, either alone or in a group, we are saying, "Come by here."

We have made the overture, taken the initiative. We have asked to sidestep our rational minds and to enter another realm. It's been said, "We are not human beings trying to live spiritual lives; rather we are spiritual beings trying to live human lives." Ritual is a way we practice remembering who we are.

Ritual and Women's Spirituality Groups

*There are no ready-made spiritual havens out there
somewhere; they are in the process of being
created by women themselves.*

JUDITH MARTIN,
Women's Studies Quarterly

*Each daily act
performed with
attention and respect
sacralized the objects
of daily use, so that
living itself could
become a ceremony.*

BARBARA WALKER
*Women's Dictionary
of Symbols and Sacred Objects*

99

Women's spirituality groups are a tool for remembering who we are, just as prayer, meditation, being in nature, singing, dancing, and reading inspirational books are such tools. What makes women's spirituality groups distinct from therapy groups or support groups or groups of just friends is that the central purpose of the group is to nourish the members' spiritual development.

Rituals and ceremonies are at the heart of women's spirituality groups. They are often the main event. They come in many shapes and sizes, from having the teakettle boiling when everyone arrives to sitting in a circle each time. Our group always sits in a circle. We wouldn't think of sitting any other way. We take turns sharing, in council fashion, without interrupting one another. These simple rituals, layered one inside another, serve to bring us back into the safety of our familiars at each meeting, back into the circle of trust and respect that we have developed over the years.

Scripted and Spontaneous

*Ritual is one of
the ways in which
humans put their
lives in perspective,
whether it be Purim,
Advent, or drawing
down the moon.
Ritual calls together
the shades and
specters in people's
lives, sorts them out,
puts them to rest.*

CLARISSA PINKOLA ESTÉS

*Women Who Run
with the Wolves*

Women's groups can do many kinds of formal rituals, ceremonies that are not spontaneous but rather carefully planned, even scripted. Formal rituals may be borrowed or modified versions of ceremonies that have been described by scholars and practitioners of the craft of rituals (see "Circle Resources" for an annotated list of books on rituals). Or they may be invented or made up, often using elements from different ritual traditions.

Along with these repeated ceremonies, a women's spirituality group also provides many opportunities for spontaneous ritual moments. A friend is suffering from cramps or a headache, so we instinctively go into a healing mode. We might touch or cradle her or simply hold her in our thoughts (especially if the person is absent from the group). One March night was unexpectedly velvety and soft, so we abandoned our indoor circle, hauled rugs out onto the back lawn, and lay on our backs, gazing up at the gnarled honey locust tree hovering above us. We entered into a mystical connection with this backyard elder, and it bestowed upon us a spontaneous blessing. We would have never expected such a gift as we walked into the meeting.

Neither spontaneous nor prepared ritual guarantees any particular kind of outcome. The ceremony that seems empty and fruitless to one may be powerful and resonant to another. The taking of communion in a Christian church may provide a powerful connection to the divine for some, whereas for others, it may be little more than an arcane ritual. Like any other phenomenon, the once holy and sacred moment can easily devolve into the rote and the routine.

Connecting and Cocreating

Rituals are essentially connective. As Diann Neu explains in her article "Women's Empowerment Through Feminist Ritual," in *Women and Therapy* magazine, this integration takes place on many levels:

> [Integration] 1) of the self with itself, as it contemplates change; 2) of the self with culture, by the use of common symbols; and 3) of the self with others, connecting celebrants into an often profound community. In ritual, doing is believing. . . . Such rites of passage . . . teach women the meaning of our existence on women's terms.

Rather than blindly accepting the precepts, rules, and paradigms of our culture, we are exploring new avenues to strengthen and empower ourselves. As Diann says, "In ritual, doing is believing." Through it, we are discovering whole new ways of being. Gradually, circle by circle, women are learning the "the meaning of our existence on women's terms." We are cocreating our own realities.

So, get loose with ceremony. Anything imaginable is possible. Get over the idea that there is a right way and a wrong way. Try things out. Experiment. Let Spirit lead into creating rituals for many occasions and situations. Let go of the idea that ceremony has to be solemn and doleful. Be playful. Spirit has a really good sense of humor, and She will appreciate yours.

One of our group members was diagnosed with breast cancer. It was at an early stage, fortunately, and so she had to

Ritual and myth are like seed crystals of new patterns that can eventually reshape culture around them.

. . . .

STARHAWK

Truth or Dare

have "only" a lumpectomy and radiation. Sandra is a brave and cheerful type, and so she soldiered on through all the treatment. When it was finally over, she said she wanted to conduct a "breast appreciation" ritual. This surprised us, since she is, by her own admission, somewhat uncomfortable with ritual. We all quickly stripped our sweaters and blouses off for a topless moment. Giddy with delight, we were able to support her in a way that was both serious and silly.

Occasions for Ritual

In our women's group, rituals celebrate occasions and mark rites of passage. We have celebrated weddings, birthdays, and births, leaving bad jobs and finding new ones, and buying homes and moving. These events are significant milestones. Creating rituals for them adds meaning and substance to our lives. We are not just living our lives from day to day. We are really living *into* our days, noting and marking the passages.

Rituals can be used to open the heart or mind, to ground, to center, to connect, to weave together, to close, to complete, to heal, to ask for help. In their wonderful book, *The Art of Ritual,* Renee Beck and Sydney Barbara Metrick identity five broad categories of ceremonies: (1) those that mark **beginnings,** such as entering into adolescence or the onset of menses; (2) those that mark **endings,** such as divorce, moving away, graduating from school; (3) those that are intended to invoke **healing,** for example, a laying-on-of-hands ceremony; (4) those that facilitate and honor **merging,** like marriage or friendship; and finally (5) those that mark **cycles,** such as equinox and solstice celebrations, which happen at the beginning of each new season of the year. Of course, these purposes are not mutually exclusive but rather overlap in many ways. For instance, all ceremonies are intended to be healing in the sense that they bring balance, perspective, and a sense of the sacred into our lives.

Ritual is a collective experience, repeated and sanctified. We perform it to remind ourselves and one another that we are not alone, that we sing in chorus.

E. M. BRONER

Honor and Ceremony

in Women's Rituals

What Makes Ceremony Meaningful?

So what is it that makes a ritual or ceremony meaningful? What is the difference between sleepwalking through a ritual and having an experience that causes you to see yourself and life itself anew? How can one bring oneself newly to the ritual moment? We believe that awareness, being in the present moment, is the key.

The sacred demands attention, requires awareness. Muslims get on their knees five times a day to remind themselves that they are servants of Allah. Catholics and Buddhists recite rosaries and intone mantras to remember their connection to the sacred. These rituals are intended to remind their practitioners of the sacred throughout their daily lives.

Human beings have short memories and even shorter attention spans. We are especially quick to forget that we can resort to the sacred at any moment. By remembering to bring our full selves and our awareness of the present moment into ritual, we enter into it in a way that is more likely to confer meaning and power.

Of course, we also need to be able to identify with the ritual in some way. It wouldn't be much fun or very useful to go to a Candlemas or Imbolc ceremony (both special days in the pagan or Wiccan tradition) if one didn't really have a basic grasp of what was going on.

Elements of Ritual

Rituals and ceremonies have an inherent, universal structure; they contain the same vital elements across traditions, cultures, and generations. These common elements are found in all rituals—Wiccan or Christian, long or short, simple or complex, formulaic or spontaneous. These elements may or may not be explicit, but more than likely they are contained within the structure of the ritual.

Element One: Intention or Purpose

Every ritual was made up at some time to serve a purpose. This purpose may or may not have been explicit at the time, but it certainly was present. Being clear about the purpose or intention of the ritual is one way to imbue it with meaning.

Our ancestors celebrated the harvest and the hunt by propitiating the gods and goddesses who oversaw these domains. Today, we might do a ritual to bring us closer in touch with our vision for the future or to help us let go of anger and

All our acts have sacramental possibilities.

FREYA STARK

Time and Tide

103

resentment over a failed relationship. We may use ritual to strengthen and prepare ourselves for a challenge or to celebrate a triumph.

In any case, we have some sort of intention for our ceremony. For ritual to be really effective we need to be clear about our intention and to state it at the outset. "This is a ritual to . . ." "We are conducting this ritual in order to . . ." It needn't be a lofty purpose. Most anything we are doing, as long as its aim is for the highest good, can be ritualized.

Setting forth the intention for the ceremony at the beginning accomplishes several things. First, it puts our minds to use in being creative. Thoughts are very powerful in the process of manifesting intentions, and telling ourselves and the universe what we want is an assertive act. The more simple and clear the intention, the better.

In addition, if more than one person is involved in the ritual, it helps to get everyone attuned to the purpose. Each person will know *why* the ceremony is being conducted and can align her own energies toward this end. Stating the intention allows anyone who feels reluctant to participate to either influence the group to change the intention or to excuse herself. Having everyone clear and in agreement with intention will greatly enhance the power of the ritual.

Ritual provides us with a way of taking responsibility for our lives through the use of the metaphoric process. At the time of a milestone or rite of passage, we can shift our focus from the minutiae of the event to the way the experience fits into the grand plan of our life.

RENEE BECK AND SYDNEY

BARBARA METRICK

The Art of Ritual

A paradox is inherent in setting forth the intention, however. Having stated the intention, we need to be open to the outcome and leave room for mystery to manifest. We are not always given to know or understand what the appropriate or most desirable outcome is for ourselves and the group.

Finally, the overall purpose of any ritual is to produce the highest good for all. We recommend adding a statement to the intention, such as, "And, finally, we ask that everything that transpires here be for the highest good of all beings." We are requesting that the ritual serve everyone spiritually, not just the people we think are most deserving. In effect, we acknowledge that our personal agendas are but a small part of a bigger picture.

Element Two: Stepping over the Threshold
into Sacred Space and Time

As we've said, ritual is a departure from our "normal" everyday consciousness. In order to make this departure, we must delineate the mundane world from the world where ceremony occurs. This delineation needs to occur both externally, in physical space, and internally in our consciousness.

When we do ritual, we may be in someone's living room or backyard, but we are not "in" the space in the conventional way. We are purposefully entering another dimension of the space, the consecrated one, and we can enter it in many ways. We might light candles or arrange altars or centerpieces with ritual objects. Some groups light incense or use a smudge stick of dried sage and other herbs to cleanse and prepare the space. You may want to lower the lights or put on some meditative music (see the "Circle Resources" for some of our favorites). Whatever you do, physically alter the space in some way to mark it as different and special.

Of course, for women's spirituality groups, establishing a circle in the space is one of the most powerful ways to "step over the threshold." In our rigid world of sharp angles, a circle of people facing one another is a powerful departure from business as usual.

Robin used to lead corporate training seminars on cultural diversity. She would purposefully set up the room so that when people entered they had to sit in a circle of preplaced chairs. This arrangement alone, before they even got into the controversial subject matter, elicited a strong reaction from many people. They joked about encounter groups and group therapy, but underneath the cloaked barbs they were reacting to the vulnerability of entering a simple circle of chairs.

Robin also worked for a year in an innovative rites-of-passage program for severely emotionally disturbed teenaged girls in the public school system. Their lives were filled with chaos, violence, self-destruction, and victimization. Many were incest survivors. The director of this program, Carol, and Robin began the academic year with ambitious plans to cover many topics, including sexuality, health, powerful heroines throughout history, and Native American and African traditions.

Every session started with an opening ritual in which the girls were asked to make a circle and state how they were feeling. For weeks they were not able even to enter the area where the circle was to be formed. Finally, they developed the capacity to enter the area and sit in a line against the farthest wall of the room. At first this seemed to be just more of their constant acting out. Over time it became clear that they came into the program so damaged that sitting in a circle facing one another was far too threatening for them. This connoted a level of being in relationship, of cooperating, of recognizing themselves and others as members of the same tribe that was way too challenging for them.

Early on, Robin began planning and choreographing a rites-of-passage initiation dance ceremony that would complete the program. After months of ignoring Robin and Carol's pleas for them to practice, the girls gathered in a mess of chaotic anxiety the day of the ceremony. Starting late, and appearing to be quite disorganized, they gradually found their way in the dance together and ended in a surprisingly graceful and very touching piece in which they really moved *together—in a circle!*

On the last day of class, the week after the initiation ceremony that signified their shift into responsible, self-respecting young womanhood, they calmly entered the circle and sat quietly listening to the teacher. It was only then that it became apparent that the essence of the curriculum for that entire year had been to develop their ability to sit in a circle. Circles are powerful. Don't take them for granted.

So the first step in any group ritual is consciously stepping over the threshold, entering the circle. Internally, we must settle down into our bodies to fully enter into ritual space. We can do this by sharing some silent minutes together, doing some easy stretches, and, most powerfully, by focusing on breathing. The deceptively simple and ancient technique of mindful breathing brings us into the moment like little else can. It is a foundational technique of meditation practice and one that we borrow for entering into ritual together. The aim is not to breathe in unison, however. Each will have her own rhythm.

Other methods of internal centering might be holding hands or chanting or toning a sound. There should be little eye contact or other interaction, and certainly no chatting. The purpose of this time is to enter into internal sacred space—to create the opportunity for each person to set aside her day, her family, and her urgent concerns and to connect within herself, to feel centered. It is a more subtle state we are seeking than the social one. We have entered into a receptive mode. We open ourselves to the wisdom, the help or the insight that we are seeking. We are going within.

Element Three: Invocation

An invocation implies that there is a power greater than that in the group whose inspiration, guidance, protection, and presence is being sought. We sometimes call on this power explicitly by name and through incantation, but being explicit is not always necessary. At its simplest level, we are inviting Spirit to make its presence known to us.

In group ceremonies, invocations can be tricky. In our women's spirituality group, we have practicing Christians alongside those who are positively allergic to Christianity; we have Goddess worshipers, followers of Native American traditions, and Buddhists. Whom would we invoke, anyway? We recommend that you find a term, a way of naming Spirit, that all can feel comfortable with. It might be God or Jesus if the group identifies as Christian, or you might want to borrow from the Native American tradition and call in the powers of the Four Directions (see the "Circle Resources" if you want a reference for this form of invocation).

Another possibility, and one that is acceptable for most people in a mixed-tradition group, is to invoke the ancestors. Calling upon the wisdom, strength, imagination, and courage of our foremothers back through time can be a wonderful way to acknowledge their legacy.

Honoring group members' ancestry can be as simple as having the leader direct people to close their eyes and to focus first on their own mothers and grandmothers. Ask people to remember and honor the strength and wisdom these women have handed down. Then suggest that people remember their great-grandmothers, and so on back up the matrilineage. Finally, people can be asked to remember all the women in their lives—heroines, role models, aunts, friends, mentors, and sisters—who have bolstered them spiritually, physically, and emotionally. Then simply give thanks for the legacy of love these women have offered. (Since some people don't have a positive relationship with their mother, make sure you

What is spoken during a ritual has a much greater impact than if spoken in normal space-time. Because of this, choose what will be said and how it will be expressed with great care.

RENEE BECK AND

SYDNEY BARBARA METRICK

The Art of Ritual

107

word the invocation so that people have room to be honest with them-selves and to claim nonbiological ancestry.)

Working with divine power requires consciousness and responsibil-ity. In ritual we are dealing with energies that may be mysterious, disem-bodied, and ethereal, but they are real nonetheless, not merely abstract symbols. There are few hard-and-fast rules to ritual, but let us tell you one guideline that Robin learned the hard way. Here is the story of Robin and Kali.

Robin and one of her colleagues were leading what was billed as an "Urban Woman's Retreat." It featured yoga and dance and ritual. In order to help participants let go of obstacles that kept them from feeling serene and centered, they invoked Kali. Kali is a Hindu goddess associated with destruction of falsehoods and obstacles to enlightenment. She is the one who comes to settle scores, to turn tables, and to set things right. Some women feel that Kali energy is rising up in these times to over-throw the vestiges of the patriarchal system.

They placed votive candles in a washtub and asked each woman to write down her personal obstacles on a small slip of paper. Each in turn stated her intention to let go of what she had written, and she dropped the slip of paper into the tub to be burned in the flames of tiny candles. Before the group knew what was happening, the fire in the tub was blazing out of control. A few of the participants got really frightened, and everyone was surprised at the force and energy present. They did get the fire under control, without any damage being done. Kali, apparently, did appear as requested.

The moral of this anecdote is, be mindful of your invoca-tions. Everything that is said and done in ceremonial space has amplified power—that is why you do it. So remain very con-scious of whom you are invoking, and invite only positive and loving energy into the space.

Element Four: The Heart of the Ceremony

The intention has been made clear, the space and time have been marked and consecrated, the invocation has been uttered. It is now time to sink into the heart of the ritual. This part of

Ritual is a tool to focus our attention on meaning; this is a skill we can develop to enhance each moment of our lives. To be truly present in our own lives is an ability we must develop if we are to continue building a foundation of relatedness and beauty in a world that can seem so divided and in pain.

RENEE BECK AND SYDNEY

BARBARA METRICK

The Art of Ritual

ritual varies widely. You may be seeking guidance, and the guidance may
come as you are in a meditative state in the form of silent promptings or
visual images. You may be led on a guided visualization by the leader of
the ritual. You may be celebrating an ecstatic movement or chant or
drumming. This may not look like receptivity. Quite the contrary!

We commonly collapse the domains of receptivity and passivity together. One of the legacies of patriarchal either-or thinking is that the
feminine principle is characterized by receptivity and that receptivity is
necessarily passive. And, of course, we have all learned that passivity is
somehow weak and not a state we want to dwell in. It is time for us to
redefine and revalue both the receptive and the passive. Some of us who
are compulsively active could use a little healthy passivity to balance out
our frenetic pace.

How about a ritual to summon the strength to say no to one of
the incessant requests for our time and energy? A ritual to celebrate the
passive, the nonreactive and unresponsive, the being part of our
nature—not just the doing, with which we are so familiar? Celebrating
being presents a real challenge to the status quo, which survives through
the voluntary efforts of so many of us. What would happen, Sonia
Johnson asks in her favorite feminist fantasy, if "during the next election
year, no women organize, raise money, stump, stamp, campaign or come
to the polls . . ."?

In ritual, we enter into a state of *active* receptivity. Witness a Haitian
voodoo ceremony, where the spirits descend and enter the bodies of the
participants. A person's entire being receives the personality,
language, and movements of the spirit that is possessing her
or him. The ceremony can last for hours, and it is anything but
passive. The voodoo ritual is used to worship the divine and
is, in fact, the primary form of Haitian worship.

Don't worry. We aren't advocating painting faces or entering a trance through the hypnotic beat of a drum (although
that does sound pretty fun)! In our group, we are a long way
from voodoo possession. The ceremonies, in fact, seem fairly
mundane. However, despite their apparent differences, the
aim of the voodoo dance and our simple chanting is the
same—to clear our minds so that we can actively receive a
glimpse of the sacred.

*To survive we must
begin to know
sacredness. The pace
which most of us lives
prevents this.*

CHRYSTOS

in *This Bridge Called My Back,*
edited by Cherrie Moraga
and Gloria Anzaldúa

Element Five: Conscious Closure

There comes a moment when we know that the heart of the ritual has come to an end. It may be a subtle shift in energy, or it may be that we have come to the end of the prepared script. Or it may be 9:30 and everyone has to pee. A ritual is not over until it has been purposefully ended.

A wobbly, loose, or unsteady closing can dissipate the energy gathered in the ritual and leave people feeling vaguely unsettled and unfinished. This is one of the trickiest parts of ritual, knowing when and how to bring closure. Trust your intuition here. You will probably make mistakes, letting things drag on or ending prematurely. You and your group will learn through experience when the moment is at hand. Doing ritual is a craft, and it takes practice.

There are many different ways of signaling the end of the ritual. Someone blows out a candle or rings a bell. The group joins hands for a few minutes or hugs. A final poem or a passage might be read or a song sung. If you have invoked some spirits or energies, you may want to thank them and bid them farewell at this point. The closing that is appropriate depends on the type of ritual that you are conducting. But it is a good idea to plan the closing ahead of time. Don't wait for the inspiration to come to you at the perfect moment, although it often will and you'll improvise the perfect closing for your ritual.

Element Six: Integration

In a society that judges self worth on productivity, it's no wonder we fall prey to the misconception that the more we do, the more we're worth.

ELLEN SUE STERN

The Indispensable Woman

It is important to make a transition back into ordinary time and space, into the circle of women sitting on the living room floor. This is a good time for a stretch break or a run to the bathroom or a mug of tea. While the special energy of the ritual has dissipated, we are still under its spell, very much affected by what transpired. This is time for integration, for digestion.

Ritual affects people in all sorts of ways. Some may be energized and excited, some may be relaxed to the point of sleepiness. Some may have received great insight, while others napped. One of our group members insists that rituals leave her cold, while others love them and think that we should do more. There is no right way to be or to feel.

Since people do react to ritual differently, choose the activities in this stage carefully. While some learn the most from discussion, others may be less verbal and will enjoy the opportunity to digest the ritual in other ways. It is just as appropriate to spend ten minutes quietly reflecting on the experience, perhaps prompted by some probing questions, as it is to have a discussion. It will depend on the group and the ritual and the moment in time. Use your intuition and be flexible. This reflection process can be as powerful an experience as the heart of the ritual itself.

Here are some questions that may help integrate the teachings of the ritual. Whether they are used in discussion, council-style sharing, artwork, or quiet reflection, these questions can be used by the leaders to prompt the group:

- What happened for you?
- Were you moved or indifferent?
- Did the ceremony elicit any strong emotion? What was it?
- Did you receive guidance and insight? Any visual images?
- Did you feel strengthened, or is it too soon to tell?

If you choose to share your experiences verbally, we recommend going around the circle so that each woman has a turn to speak without interruption. We hear ourselves in others, and our learnings are amplified as we go around the circle. Another option is to have some art materials on hand. Let people draw an image that represents their experience and then share based on their image. Or people could journal and simply read from their writing.

Finally, you may want to ask people to reflect on the implications of their experience and of their learnings from the ceremony. Is there any way that what happened here can translate into your daily life? Does it inform some decision you are trying to make? Does it indicate some action that might be taken?

It is not necessary or even appropriate to expect that people will "use" everything that happens in ritual. A ritual is not

The end of a thing,
is never the end,
something is always
born like
a year or a baby.

LUCILLE CLIFTON

Everett Anderson's Year

a linear process. However, if the ritual was effective, if it was powerful, it may very well lend itself to a practical application. One may see a need to spend more time nurturing the body. One may come to recognize that quiet time is incredibly important and decide to carve some out. One may realize a hunger for some aesthetic pleasures, some beauty, and plan to go to a gallery in the coming week. Or one may even feel the call to make a major life decision—to marry, to divorce, to move. Asking the questions may coax some additional insight out of the ceremony.

However you choose to enact it, the integration is, in effect, another vital element, one that is crucial to discovering all that there is to learn. And ritual thus becomes not only a way for us to worship, but also an opportunity to learn more about how mystery manifests itself in our lives.

*What is holiness but
wholeness?*

....

STELLA MORTON

Shadow of Wings

Ritual Planning Guide

RITUAL ELEMENT   **GUIDING QUESTIONS**

General Questions

How much time do you have for the ceremony?

How many people are you expecting?

What space would be appropriate?

Do you want to create an altar or centerpiece to focus the attention of the participants?

What symbolic objects do you want to display?

Do you want people to bring something to add to the altar?

Do you want to use music?

Is there a particular scent (incense or aromatherapy) that would enhance the ritual?

Are there specific colors to wear or to use in decorating that will fit the intention and the mood?

In what way could you bring the natural world or season of the year into the ritual?

Element One: Intention

What is motivating you to conduct this ceremony?

What is your purpose in conducting this ceremony?

Element Two: Stepping over the Threshold

Is the space you are using set apart in some away?

Are you likely to have interruptions or distractions?

Can you eliminate or minimize these?

Do you want to "cleanse" the space with sage or incense?

Can you create a circle in the space?

Do you want to do some deep breathing or stretching to help people make the shift into sacred space?

Element Three: Invocation

Is a particular kind of invocation appropriate for your ceremony?

> Invoke the ancestors?

> Call in the four directions?

> Ask for the healing power of the elements?

> Ask for healing? Knowledge? Insight?

Is there a reading that speaks deeply to your intention?

Remember to request that only the highest energies be present and to ask for the highest good for all beings.

Element Four: Heart of the Ceremony

Keeping your intention in mind, what could you do here that symbolizes your purpose?

What actions could you take that would embody your quest?

Could you involve one or more of the elements in this part of the ritual?

> Water: Wash yourself or someone else, drink

Air: Blow on something, breathe in

Fire: Burn something you have written down, light candles

Earth: Bury something, hold a stone

Element Five: Conscious Closure

How do you envision ending the ritual?

Is there a reading, a song, a poem you want to share?

Element Six: Integration

How do you see people "digesting" the ritual?

Do you want to provide paper and art materials for drawing?

Do you want to ask for silence?

Is there some sort of physical movement that would help people integrate?

Do you want to ask the list of integration questions directly?

What happened for you?

Were you moved or indifferent?

Did the ceremony elicit any strong emotion? What was it?

Did you receive any guidance or insight? Any visual images?

Did you feel strengthened, or is it too soon to tell?

. . . .

Reclaiming ceremony is a deceptively powerful act. Instead of abdicating authority and control to others (generally men), we are taking responsibility for finding our own way. Women's spirituality groups, and ritual in particular, are a profound way for women to get on with the art of living fully. When we are ready to take the reins of our own lives, we find the energy to move beyond our limits.

In this chapter, we have invited you to see ceremony in a different way. It is our hope that ritual will take on a new meaning and role in

your life as something alive and juicy rather than dead and stale. As
Barbara Ardinger states in *A Woman's Book of Rituals,* when it is engaged
in consciously, "instead of ruts, ritual can create paths."

Sample Ceremonies

We wanted to share with you some of the rituals that we have created
or participated in. As you can see, they are user-friendly. They don't require huge amounts of preparation, memorization, or burned offerings
to ancient deities. If you want to pursue your ritualizing further, turn
to the resource guide, where we have annotated some of our favorite
books and resources. Remember, the main thing is to approach ritual
with a mixture of playfulness and respect, clear intention, and open-
mindedness.

Weaving a Web

At some level, we know we are all interconnected. This ritual reminds
us of interconnection in a simple yet profound way. We have done this at
birthdays or as the closing ritual at the end of a workshop. We start in a
circle with a ball of string or, preferably, brightly colored yarn. The person who starts holds on to one end and passes or tosses the ball to another person, saying how she feels connected to her or, alternatively,
how they met. This continues until the web is woven and everyone is
connected. One cautionary note: this works best when everyone in the
group knows one another at least a little.

Seeking Wisdom

This ritual is one that Sally and Robin participated in at a women's
wilderness retreat at Ghost Ranch in New Mexico. It was conducted
around a bonfire, but that is not a prerequisite! Each woman wrote on a
piece of paper a question that she had been wrestling with, folded the
paper, and placed it in a hat. One by one, each woman drew a question
that someone else had posed and answered it without knowing who had
asked it. Unexpected wisdom emerged from such randomness.

Birthday Ceremony

Birthdays are wonderful times for rituals, but the last thing most of us need is presents, more stuff. At our age, our closets and cupboards and drawers are full enough. So we devised a simple ritual to celebrate our birthdays without having to spend a dime. Each person gets an index card and writes a few words describing the unique gifts that the birthday girl brings to the group. Each person in turn reads the card she has written and presents it as her gift.

Hanukkah Ritual

One of our friends, Tamar, belongs to a Jewish women's spirituality group. The group meets on the new moon of each month. At Hanukkah, a holiday that celebrates freedom, each woman brought in a family menorah. Displayed on a table, the menorahs were each unique in design and yet carried a common symbology. As each women lit the nine candles of her family's menorah, she made a statement about freedom. By the end of the sharing, the room was ablaze with the over 180 candles, full of power and bright light.

A Blessing Way

Adapted from a Native American tradition, a Blessing Way is wonderful way to honor and nurture a woman who is about to go through a major life passage. Native Americans used the ceremony when a woman is about to be married and or ready to give birth. It can be easily adapted for other rites of passage as well.

The leader begins by stating the intention to acknowledge and serve the woman of honor. There may be readings about giving birth or marriage. The role that the community of women play in one another's lives is evoked. Then all present take turns washing and drying (if there is time) and combing and brushing the honoree's hair. Together they arrange her hair in a distinctively different way than the usual style. Flowers and combs are used to beautify her hair. Of course, everyone comments on her beauty during this time.

The woman of honor is then gently massaged, as every woman present takes a hand or foot or head or shoulder and gently rubs. At some point, the traditional ceremony calls for washing the feet of the honoree in warm, scented water and rubbing them with cornmeal. This feels incredibly good, works off rough skin, and leaves the feet very soft. Once the feet are dried, sweet-smelling lotion can be applied.

Finally, each woman presents a symbolic object, such as a poem, a song, or anything else that expresses her blessings for the birth, the new baby, or the marriage. Or, each woman can place a handmade or specially selected bead on a string. The beads will carry the unique blessings of each woman. If the woman is giving birth, she may want to hold the beads during her labor and delivery.

The ceremony is simple, sweet, and incredibly nurturing to the woman being honored and to everyone else, too. Through this ritual we mark a passage in someone else's life, and we remind ourselves of those passages in our own lives. And maybe most important, we take the too rare opportunity to treat our bodies as the temples they are.

A Blessing Way variation that we have tried is to have everyone choose a partner and take turns doing her partner's hair and massaging her partner's feet, as described above. It allows for more participation in a big group, and it does nothing to detract from the spotlight being on the intended woman.

A New Year's Ceremony

A few years ago Robin's sister Clair designed and led this simple and powerful ritual to begin a new year. We sat in the dark, except for the light of many, many candles of all sizes. Beginning with a guided visualization that focused on seeing ourselves as all that we were in that moment, we were encouraged to let go of our limiting ideas and fears and imagine ourselves in our full potential. We then went into a journaling exercise in which we wrote down our goals for our lives in the next year, capturing not just things we wanted to have but also the ways we wanted our lives to be—calm and peaceful, having lots of fun, and so forth.

Next, we shared these goals with one another. Clair suggested that we speak the goals in present tense, as if they existed now. "My life is peaceful, and I have lots of time for myself." "I feel fulfilled in my work, and I make a very prosperous living at it." Declaring personal goals in public can be very confronting. If we keep our dreams to ourselves, it isn't as embarrassing when we don't accomplish them. But when we promise to others that we will do something, the stakes get higher. There is power in sharing our goals with our trusted friends. Our friends add to our energy and intention to create the life we want.

The last part of the ritual was the most profound. Each person was asked to take a small piece of paper and write down one barrier, one thing that most gets in the way of her having what she wants in life. Usually, this one thing is a limiting belief, some idea, some fear that keeps us from reaching out and grabbing all that is there for us.

Each person then took turns stating what she had written on her slip of paper and telling the group that she was ready to relinquish that obstacle. For instance, "I, Laura, now relinquish the belief that I am not lovable enough to have a great partner." Or, "I, Jill, let go of the fear that I will be rejected if I am truly myself." As we spoke our fears, we crumpled the paper and put it in the fire.

The ritual ended with a quiet time as each person saw herself receiving what she asked for. Then Clair asked Spirit for assistance for each person to achieve her dreams.

. . . .

Endless adventures are to be had through ritual. The suggestions we've presented here are just the beginning. We recommend Barbara Ardinger's book, *A Woman's Book of Rituals and Celebrations;* Barbara Walker's book, *Women's Rituals;* and Jennifer Louden's books, *The Woman's Comfort Book* and *The Woman's Retreat Book.* Not only are they all fun to read, they will inspire your imagination to create ceremonies that fit your occasion and mood exactly.

Juicy Themes for Drawing Closer

*I*n our group we organize our meetings around themes or topics, since we like having a focus for the evening. Based on this focus, we plan simple activities and rituals. The topic is usually chosen by the two women who have volunteered to be conveners, or mothers, for that meeting. They may choose something of interest to them or allow themselves to be guided by group members' requests. Frequently, there is no clear choice for a theme until a few days before the meeting. At that point, we get a call from a mother, who announces the theme and asks us to bring relevant materials or reflections.

This chapter contains the themes for group meetings divided into four categories according to the longevity of the group. Groups that have just begun meeting tend to do better with less sensitive topics, while those that have had time to develop more trust and intimacy can address more potentially volatile themes.

THEMES FOR STARTING GROUPS

Childhood Religion: The Faith of Our Fathers
Awakening into the Natural World
Creativity as a Practice
A Long Lineage: Our Spiritual Foremothers

THEMES FOR MORE INTIMATE GROUPS

Food, Glorious Food
Our Mothers, Ourselves
Beauty: Mirror, Mirror on the Wall
New Paths to Power
Giving Birth

THEMES FOR LONG-TERM GROUPS

Menstruation: The Bleeding Time
Money: Making It and Spending It
Menopause: The Wisdom Years
Climaxes and Contradictions: Talking About Sex
Death and Dying

THEMES FOR ANY GROUP, ANYTIME

The Seasons: Reconnecting to the Rhythms
of the Earth
Potpourris and Pajama Parties

Choosing a Topic

Meeting themes can be anything of interest to the women in the group. Don't be put off if people suggest things that don't seem "spiritual" to you at all. If people enter the meeting with a willing attitude, the theme will work. It will work because all aspects of our lives are related to our spirits, even though we may not always see the connection. It will work because, if the topic is approached candidly, people will learn more about themselves, and if they share those discoveries, a sense of spiritual connection will deepen.

While there is no such thing as a bad topic, there is such a thing as a topic approached superficially. The technical term for this phenomenon is chitchat. There is nothing wrong with chitchat. We love it, and we have added thirty minutes on to the beginning of each meeting, before we sit in a circle, just so we can catch up with one another's lives. How-ever, we recommend that once we get into the circle itself, chitchat be kept to a minimum. It helps to set this time and this group of people apart from the rest of our social life.

We can chat anywhere. But we can't, just anywhere, have an honest exploration of a compelling topic in which we can speak as long as we like and be listened to intently. Nor do we often have the opportunity to learn from the innermost thoughts and feelings of other women we re-spect. The bottom line is "make the time count." Go into the topic, ei-ther as a leader or a participant, candidly and wholeheartedly.

Focusing the Topic

Once you choose a theme, it's up to you and your co-mother to develop it. It's your baby. Use the opportunity to tap your fertile imagination. There is no right way to treat a theme. In fact, introducing or engaging with a theme in an unusual way can bring an entirely new light to the topic for you and for the women you are leading.

We suggest sitting down with your co-mother and deciding on an as-pect of the theme you want to explore in the meeting. Let's say you are going to be dealing with childhood religious experience. Do you want people to tell their stories, or do you want to foster a discussion? Two different approaches. Most interesting topics are so complex and multi-faceted that you could have ten meetings on them and barely scratch the surface. So limit your exploration to the facet of the topic that interests you most. Let's say that you have decided that you want to hear women tell their stories about going to Sunday school. Then begin to brainstorm. Do you want to give them a leading question to think about ahead of time? Do you want to use crayons and coloring books? Do you want peo-ple to bring in mementos (the Sunday school attendance award, the bat mitzvah commentary)? Verbalize any and every idea. Play with each other's energy and imaginations. Spend at least twenty minutes or so re-ally letting loose before focusing in on the ideas that most appeal to you.

You may notice that we have suggested that you follow your own in-tuition rather than try to figure out what will please everyone in the group. As conveners, you have the chance to take the group where you want to go—to let your style, your interests, your preferences guide the way. Most of us were raised to place others' interests ahead of our own in all situations. We can't even imagine being so selfish as to take the whole group on a journey that fascinates us. Please, *be just that selfish*. Rather than figuring out what will make the group happy, figure out what you want to do. In every case we have seen so far, the group is glad to go there. Often, people mention that one of the best things about rotating leadership is that it allows them to experience the themes in ways they never would have thought of for themselves.

Structuring the Meeting

The mothers usually develop one or two questions to get everyone thinking. They call ahead and give us these questions. They may also ask us to wear a certain color or especially comfortable clothes or to bring something for the altar or centerpiece. The mothers then plan the flow of the evening. Here are some questions for you to consider when planning the meeting:

- Will you open with a reading or silence or some stretching?
- Will you include a ritual of some sort? Will you use music?
- How will the sharing take place—in pairs, small groups, or all together in the circle?
- What about nonverbal activities, like drawing or clay work, massage or movement?
- How will you bring the evening to a close?

Dealing with Sensitive Topics

Many topics are more sensitive than one might expect. For example, our group has some pretty ardent supporters of home-birthing, and when we dealt with the topic of childbirth, things got a bit touchy. People hated to think they "did it wrong" by choosing to have a hospital birth or by accepting anesthesia. It's important not to find a "right" answer or position for the group to coalesce around. The point is to engage with the questions and to consider that these arenas—new to some of us, familiar territory to others—are worth our time and energy. We need to create a safe context for exploring rather than debating.

Be mindful of where you, the leaders, draw the line between what is speakable and what is not. The leaders' degree of candidness and willingness to self-disclose will set the stage. We advise the leaders to acknowledge the tenderness of the subject in opening the session and to remind people of their promise to honor confidentiality, in order to create a safe environment.

In this chapter we have gathered up some of the most interesting, provocative, and successful themes we have used in our group over the last four years and some that we haven't yet explored. Our suggestions are meant, not as a prescription, but as a jumping-off place for your ideas. Every one of the topics we present here could be approached in many different ways. Our intent is to spark your imagination, both for what kinds of things can be used as themes and for how to engage with the themes themselves.

A Guide to Using the Rest of This Chapter

This chapter is designed to give you a sense of the breadth of subjects available to your group. It is by no means definitive or comprehensive. It will feed your creativity and give you a place to begin to develop themes that are accessible, compelling, and challenging. The topics are ordered by the degree of challenge they have presented to us, so the topics suggested for new groups come first, followed by the ones more suitable for long-term groups or groups in which intimacy has developed quickly. Feel free to try them out of sequence!

Under the heading of each theme, we present an overall context. Next, you will find **Guiding Questions.** You may want to ask yourselves some of them as you are planning the topic. Do they provoke a response in you? Do you find yourself challenged, feeling nervous or excited? Do you want to go further? These are signs that this theme may be a good choice for you. In addition, the questions can be used as the guiding questions for council sharing in the meeting itself. In any case, we provide far more questions than you could use in one meeting; choose the ones that call to you, or make up your own.

Following the Guiding Questions is a section on **Readings.** Clearly, every topic leads one to a bibliography of many fascinating books and articles. Our intent here is not to provide a comprehensive resource list on each subject but rather a few selected books that are full of useful, pungent, and provocative short readings on the matter at hand. You may want to browse through them to find a relevant piece that sets just the right tone to introduce your topic.

Next, we have included a section entitled **Suggested Activities.** Again, these are just a place to start. You could never do them all in one meeting. These are suggestions for activities, or even parts of rituals, that can enliven and bring an experiential aspect to your meeting.

Finally, we suggest **Altar Craft** for each topic. One of our group's favorite practices is the creating of a centerpiece, or altar, in the circle. *Altar* is a freighted word. Some of the women in your group may object to using it outside of a church setting. We first encountered questions about altars as we were preparing a proposal for the first "Sacred Circles" gathering that we helped to organize at the Washington National Cathedral. We suggested a workshop intended to help women create their own personal altars, and our suggestion was vetoed by the cathedral. The word *altar* actually derives from the Latin, where it meant a housewife's hearth. Women in many cultures have used altars to create sacred space in the home. In Gujarat, India, housewives go out at dawn and paint religious symbols on their walls and doors, turning their whole houses into offerings to the divine. Russians have icons in their homes, and the Vietnamese have ancestor shrines, with flowers, candles, and incense.

The centerpiece, or altar, in our group is designed by the mothers for each meeting and generally bears some relation to the meeting's topic. It both beautifies and consecrates the space. Often, people are asked ahead of time to bring something relevant to the theme to place on the altar, so it becomes a collaborative aesthetic creation. In addition, the altar is a place where we can bring our attention to seasonal and cyclical matters. Is it spring? How can the resplendence of spring be woven into that evening's theme? We offer a few simple suggestions to express the essence of your meeting in your centerpiece or altar.

Themes for Starting Groups

Childhood Religion: The Faith of Our Fathers

It is a rare family that can trace back beyond two or three generations and not find that their predecessors were deeply immersed in the attitudes and values of one of the male-oriented religions. It is for this reason that religious pressures are not as far from us as we might prefer to think.

MERLIN STONE,
When God Was a Woman

Childhood religion was one of the first topics our group ever tried. Exploring this subject early on is a good idea for several reasons. First, it helps the group get a sense of context—where we all come from in terms of our religious backgrounds.

Second, it helps group members to put on the table some of the rough edges, the sore places, they may have brought with them into the group with regard to religion and spirituality. For instance, one woman in our group had a negative experience of being brought up Catholic, with a parochial education. She told her story, and now we all know where and why she is struggling with it. If your group is church or synagogue based, people may be a little more reluctant to share negative religious experiences they had as children.

We found it simply amazing to learn how varied were our experiences. In our group, three of us, Robin and her sister, Clair, and Elizabeth were brought up in Southern Baptist homes. For Robin, this was quite traumatic, for Liz, quite the contrary. One of our members, Allison, hadn't gone to church as a child. She married a Jew, keeps kosher and is enthusiastically raising her three sons in keeping with Jewish traditions. For her, the lack of a dogmatic upbringing may have made it easier to convert to Judaism. More differences. Seeing the diversity of experience allows people both to validate and claim their own experience, and at the same time to see clearly how differently people experience this part of their upbringing. Women also begin to see that, more often than not, the religious exposure they had as children was one where men were in positions of power and spiritual authority.

◎ GUIDING QUESTIONS

1. What was your religious upbringing like?
2. How did you feel about this when you were a child?
3. How does this upbringing influence the person you are today?
4. How have you brought up your children?

◎ READINGS

A God Who Looks Like Me, by Patricia Lynn Reilly
Beyond God the Father, by Mary Daly
The Feminine Face of God, by Sherry Ruth Anderson and Patricia
    Hopkins
Models of God, by Sallie McFague

◎ SUGGESTED ACTIVITIES

1. Leave plenty of time to do council-style sharing about each person's childhood experience of religion. Let people describe this in as much detail as they can.
2. Explore the question of how each person's current life is influenced by her religious upbringing.
3. Conduct a journaling exercise in which everyone writes the gifts she received from her religious upbringing. Sharing with the whole group could occur at this point. Then have each person write down all the lessons she has had to unlearn, or is still in the process of unlearning, with regard to her religious upbringing. Again, people may want to share these insights with the group.

◎ ALTAR CRAFT

Arrange mementos and keepsakes of early childhood religious experience: first communion dresses and veils, candelabras, dreidels, confirmation programs, Sunday school books, bat mitzvah programs, crosses, medals.

Awakening into the Natural World

*A tree is an aerial garden, a botanical migration from the sea,
from those earliest plants, the seaweeds; it is a purchase on
crumbled rock, on ground. The human, standing, is only a
different upsweep and articulation of cells. How treelike we are,
how human the tree.*

GRETEL EHRLICH, *River History*

Both of us grew up in the suburbs. To us, being out in nature meant climbing on our bikes or learning the names of birds for a Girl Scout merit badge or camping out in the backyard. In fact, it verged on the socially unacceptable to be too interested in nature. It just wasn't a girl thing. We remember all too vividly the poison ivy blisters, the sunburned shoulders, and the insect bites. Robin mentored a teenage girl who is terrified by the idea of doing anything outside, even taking a walk in the countryside. Robin continually tried to lure her out.

When women connect with one another in a spiritual context, they gradually become more connected with the natural world as well. This is one of the hallmarks of women's spirituality.

We have all had tremendous help in reconnecting with nature. Inspired by writers like Annie Dillard, Diane Ackerman, and Terry Tempest Williams, we have started going back outside for the sheer ecstasy of it. We are gardening and composting, river rafting, rock climbing, and just lying on our backs and stargazing. We are starting to reexperience our organic connection to the larger whole. We are being spoken to by the great natural forces swirling around and through us. We are becoming reenchanted by the trees, flowers, rocks, birds, clouds, and cliffs.

Time and again, our group has provided a setting for us to experience and discuss our longing for this sacred connection. You will find that even if your group is not working with a nature theme, meetings will include many reminders that we humans are part of a much larger living world. However, we do suggest that periodically you choose to focus explicitly on the natural world as a dimension of our spirituality.

◎　GUIDING QUESTIONS

1. How have you been separated from the natural world?

2. What are your fears about being in nature?

3. What keeps you inside?

4. What was your family of origin's connection to the natural world?

5. How have you reconnected with nature?

6. How does nature speak to you most powerfully? When do you feel most connected?

7. As a child, did you ever witness or participate in cruelty to animals? How did that feel? How does it feel now? How do you think it influenced you?

◎　READINGS

Woman and Nature, by Susan Griffin
Pilgrim at Tinker Creek, by Annie Dillard
Desert Quartet: An Erotic Landscape, by Terry Tempest Williams
Sisters of the Earth: Women's Prose and Poetry about Nature, edited by
　　Lorraine Anderson
A Natural History of the Senses, by Diane Ackerman
New and Selected Poems, by Mary Oliver

◎　SUGGESTED ACTIVITIES

1. Have an evening on trees—just trees.

2. Meet outside under the stars.

3. Bring the outside inside, with branches and blossoms.

4. Do a wilderness solo for a few hours, then come back together and share. If you live in the city, you may have to go to a nearby park or urban garden. Your "wilderness" doesn't have to be wild.

5. Create a guided meditation to heal the separation we feel from nature. For instance, ask questions about how people experienced animals and other nature when they were children. Then ask about when that connection changed and how it changed. Ask what the loss of connection with nature has cost people in their lives. Finally, have the meditation focus on healing that separation, and let an inner guide suggest ways to heal the split.

6. Find some pithy nature quotes, read one at a time to your group, and invite people to journal in a stream of consciousness in response to the quote. Then read your writing out loud to one another.

7. Share your favorite poems about nature.

8. Bring in your Girl Scout merit badges and share what you remember.

9. Share childhood memories of being in nature.

10. Listen together to one of the many nature sound CDs available. Or just have a CD playing in the background, such as the sound of frogs croaking or waves crashing on a shore.

◉   **ALTAR CRAFT**

Let your imagination run free: rocks, leaves, shells, dirt. Have all the natural elements on the altar: water, air, fire, and earth. Make a pretend campfire indoors. Toast marshmallows. Once our group rigged a tentlike structure with blankets and all crawled inside.

Creativity as a Practice

To live a creative life, we must lose our fear of being wrong.

JOSEPH CHILTON PEARCE

Most of us were brought up to believe that creativity was a gift that you either were given or not. Sally started being self-conscious about her drawing when she hit first grade. She finally realized once and for all in the eighth grade that she definitely hadn't received this particular gift when an "art" teacher criticized one of her drawings. She spent the next forty years feeling certain that she wasn't creative. It wasn't until just before her fiftieth birthday that she began to reclaim her creativity, even though her creative juices had long been flowing. When she finally emerged out of this shadowy state of unknowing and disbelieving, she recognized that she was an accomplished artist in the fields of cooking, calligraphy, and conversation. From this realization, she began to branch out into writing, gardening, and drumming. Now she regards many domains as avenues for creative exploration.

Just what do we mean by the *practice* of creativity? We believe that creativity is the birthright of everyone, not just the immortal few (and incidentally, why are those few "great" artists exhibited in the top museums of the world almost all European men?). But in order to develop creativity, we must be actively and consciously engaged with it. Lots of activities stifle creativity; watching television and overworking are among the most virulent.

With creativity, it is the process rather than the product that is most important. This may sound counterintuitive to those of us who equate creative ability with artistic production. But being in the flow of a creative impulse has an ecstatic dimension. If you get all hung up in trying to make something beautiful or perfect, you will probably experience anxiety rather than ecstasy. Perfectionism is not what we are talking about here!

The practice of creativity involves recognizing and letting go of obstacles to creative expression. Remember all those remarks you heard and internalized? "Your sister is a really good artist. She has talent." All the old tapes have to be replaced with positive feedback from ourselves.

Most of the time, when we are engaged with our creativity, we are doing it strictly for our own benefit. Depending on your conditioning, this can feel downright selfish. It requires passive receptivity to ideas and concepts as well as active imagination. It sometimes asks us to take risks, exposing ourselves to criticism or ridicule. In the practice of creativity there is really no such thing as a mistake.

Every child is an artist. The problem is how to remain one as [she] grows up.

PABLO PICASSO

Last year both of us stumbled upon *The Artist's Way: A Spiritual Path to Higher Creativity,* by Julia Cameron. This is modeled on the twelve steps of recovery, and central to it is the notion that we are vehicles through which creativity comes from some higher power. We worked our way diligently through the chapters and exercises—lots of reflecting, brainstorming, affirmations, questions. We embarked on the practice of taking "artist dates" and writing "morning pages," three pages each and every morning. It seemed terribly daunting at first, especially the week of no reading (!), but we quickly began to reap the benefits. Our confidence in our own creative muscles had diminished over the years, and we were beginning to stretch and tone them, preparing them for some heavy lifting. All of this gave us tremendous sustenance as we embarked on writing this book. We can't recommend *The Artist's Way* highly enough. In fact, many women's groups have formed specifically for the purpose of working through *The Artist's Way* material together.

Creativity is an especially good theme for groups that are just beginning. It's not as highly charged as many of the other topics, and it is definitely something that all will be eager to explore, even though they may think they are not "creative" people. Hopefully, they will have started to change their opinion of themselves after this meeting!

> *The imagination needs moodling,— long, inefficient, happy idling, dawdling and puttering.*
>
> ················
>
> BRENDA UELAND
>
> *If You Want to Write*

◉ GUIDING QUESTIONS

1. What were you told as a child about your artistic ability? How did this affect you?

2. What obstacles have you noticed to your creative expression? How do you define creativity? What have you told yourself about your creativity?

3. How does your inner artist manifest herself? Another way of asking the same question is, Which activities give you the most pleasure? When are you the happiest?

4. Where and how does your perfectionism show up?

5. What have you always wanted to try and were afraid to?

6. How are you learning to listen to yourself, to your deepest longings?

7. What conditions, settings, or circumstances are the most conducive to your creativity?

◎ READINGS

The Artist's Way, by Julia Cameron
The Vein of Gold, also by Julia Cameron
Centering, by M. C. Richards
Bird by Bird, by Anne Lamott
The Four-Fold Way, by Angeles Arrien
Meditations for Women Who Do Too Much, by Anne Wilson Schaef
Drawing on the Right Side of the Brain, by Betty Edwards
Creative Visualization, by Shakti Gawain
Writing Down the Bones, by Natalie Goldberg

◎ SUGGESTED ACTIVITIES

1. Have women draw a representation of their bodies, drawing or coloring where they physically experience blockages in creativity. Share about these.

2. Lead a guided visualization where each woman imagines herself in the throes of the creative experience. What is she doing? Where is she doing it? How does she feel?

3. Make a group art piece and then destroy it, burn it, or bury it, like the Tibetan monks who sweep away their intricate colored sand mandalas after they have finished them.

4. After a warm-up, do some gentle improvisational dancing. See what the group creates together.

5. Have women bring in something they have made or written or sung for a creative, not competitive, show-and-tell.

6. Create a ritual where women share their creative blocks, writing them down on pieces of paper, then offering them to the fire.

7. Do an exercise from *The Artist's Way* or *Drawing on the Right Side of the Brain.*

8. Create a ritual to exorcise blocks to creativity. This one is based on *The Artist's Way*. Have each person start by saying aloud something like "I am a brilliant creative artist." Then have everyone write on a slip of paper the first negative thought that comes to mind in response to this affirmation. Repeat this ten to fifteen times. When everyone has made a list of all her negative self-criticisms, burn these lists together. You might want to read your lists aloud, all at the same time.

◎   **ALTAR CRAFT**

Ask women to bring in objects they consider the fruits of their creativity. Each woman then places her objects on the altar and tells why she chose them. Or ask members to bring in their favorite beautiful object and ceremonially place it in the center.

A Long Lineage: Our Spiritual Foremothers

Sons branch out, but one woman leads to another.

MARGARET ATWOOD

Remembering and reclaiming our female spiritual lineage is important work for us. We need all the inspiration and anchoring we can get. Some of us undoubtedly have had our own heroines. Sally's early ones were Helen Keller, Margaret Mead, and Eleanor Roosevelt, and Robin's were Helen Keller, Joan of Arc, and Jane Fonda. But equally, if not more, important are the ones we actually know in our lives.

Most of us probably had few spiritual women role models when we were growing up, at least models we consciously wanted to emulate. But a strange transformation takes place as we age and gain a little more perspective. We start to appreciate those women who had a positive impact on us, even though we may not have realized it at the time. The mother who seemed an intervening and controlling presence for a gawky adolescent may turn out to have taught us some important lessons, too. It's the mothers, grandmothers, aunts,

There's no love so pure it can thrive without its incarnations.

· · · · · · · · · · · · · ·

MICHELE MURRAY

133

teachers, nuns, and family friends who have the most immediate impact on us, and they are the ones we most need to reclaim and honor as our spiritual foremothers.

Often, these foremothers have died. One of Sally's greatest personal influences was her great-grandmother, Nanny, who lived in a little town in Texas. When Sally was two her family moved from Texas. Rarely thinking about Nanny during her childhood, Sally probably saw her great-grandmother only ten more times in her life. Nanny died in 1957. But in retrospect, Nanny played a significant role in showing an alternative option for spiritual expression. She was a gardener rather than a churchgoer, and her iris and narcissus bulbs were her implements of worship. It's never too late to recognize and reclaim a spiritual foremother. Future generations are depending on us to pass down their legacy.

Grandmother consciousness opens a woman to images of the past, to the face of the future, and to the symbolic pattern of a woman's life.

NAOMI RUTH LOWINSKY

GUIDING QUESTIONS

1. When you were growing up, who were your role models? Why?

2. Did you have any models for spiritually evolved women? Did any appear in your actual lineage?

3. Do you claim any spiritual foremothers now that you didn't recognize as a child?

4. If you could be in contact with any of your dead women ancestors for spiritual nurture, whom would you choose? How has this woman affected your life?

5. Whom have you not yet claimed as a spiritual foremother? What stands in the way of claiming her?

READINGS

Poems in *Cries of the Spirit*, edited by Marilyn Sewell
"Mother of Mothers: The Power of the Grandmother in the Female Psyche," in *To Be A Woman: The Birth of the Conscious Feminine*, edited by Connie Zweig

Return of the Great Goddess, edited by Burleigh Muten

The Dinner Party: A Symbol of Our Spiritual Heritage, by Judy Chicago

◎ **SUGGESTED ACTIVITIES**

1. Introduce your spiritual foremothers to the group, and invent a ritual where you invite them into the circle. Share how you came to reconnect with their legacy.

2. Tell one another stories of times you remember with your foremothers. Try to imagine what their lives would be like if they were alive today. What wise counsel would they be offering you?

3. Share about your public role models (not in your biological family), such as historical figures. Women of different ages may have different public role models. Acknowledge and enjoy the generational differences.

4. In what ways would you like to be regarded as a role model?

5. Create a guided visualization where each person takes a question to someone in her spiritual lineage and receives wisdom.

6. Show Donna Read's film *The Burning Times* (available on video). Many of us may have had ancestors who were persecuted and killed for ostensibly practicing witchcraft but more probably because they threatened the patriarchal status quo.

7. Conduct a ritual to remember those who have gone before and who have been forgotten (this might include the millions of women killed during the burning times).

◎ **ALTAR CRAFT**

Make a shrine to your spiritual foremothers with pictures of them, gifts they may have given you, family Bibles, books. You might want to place underneath everything a shawl of theirs or an afghan a grandmother knitted. Or, place on the altar an object that symbolizes something for which you would like to be remembered.

Themes for More Intimate Groups

Food, Glorious Food

*Once I went to a potluck supper for the 4-H club my children
belonged to, and seventeen of the twenty women on the Food
Committee brought quivering green-and-pink molded
"salads" striped with marshmallows and store-bought
mayonnaise. Their hardworking rancher husbands
circled the three tuna-noodle casseroles like hungry
coyotes until the desserts, packaged cake mixes
heaped with aerosol Fudge Whippo,
were served forth.*

M. F. K. FISHER,
Dubious Honors

Food is another loaded topic, especially for us women. Why is it that
more of us women seem to "live to eat" than do the men in our lives,
who "eat to live"? Many of us have an actual relationship with food. We
adore it. We hate it. We are obsessed with it. It's our best friend one day
and our worst enemy the next. How very strange that our natural nurturing function has turned into such a double-edged sword, and one we
are falling on all the time.

Some in our group have struggled with bulimia and compulsive
overeating, and others have engaged in rounds of yo-yo dieting. Can we
possibly help ourselves to heal our relationship with food? We think we
can. By focusing on the healthy aspects of our relationship with food, we
begin to restore some sense of balance. Enjoying a slice of warm crusty
sourdough bread, slathered with something yummy, is a
healthy indulgence. But if we are bingeing every other day, we
can never let ourselves enjoy even the modest treat; we will
feel too guilty about the big binge, which we didn't really
enjoy anyway. Human beings were not made to starve and deprive ourselves.

Bringing the shadow side of our relationship with food into
the light is profoundly healing. Virtually all women we know

*Eating is never so
simple as hunger.*

ERICA JONG
"The Catch," Becoming Light

136

relate to food in unhealthy ways at times, and everyone thinks she is the only one. Well, the fact is, we are not alone. Ambivalence and struggle with food are some of the most common experiences American women have. Talking about it loosens it grip on us.

And then there's the lovely side of food, the fun side, the artistic side, the nurturing side. The cooking and the sharing of our food. Our group hardly ever shares this pleasure together. Our schedules are such that most of us fly in at the last minute, already having grabbed a bite somewhere along the way. We wish that our lives were a little less complicated and that we could have the occasional potluck. We recommend that you treat yourselves occasionally to the delight of preparing food for one another.

*As she is a woman,
and as she is an
American, she was
dieting.*

················

KATHERINE WHITEHORN
"Meeting Mary McCarthy,"
in *The Observer*

◎ **GUIDING QUESTIONS**

1. How would you characterize your relationship to food?

2. How do you see food—as your friend or your enemy?

3. Do you "eat to live" or "live to eat"?

4. Do you use food to anesthetize yourself? How do you use or abuse food?

5. How was food treated in your family of origin?

6. How does food give you pleasure? Pain?

7. What are you favorite foods, your comfort foods?

8. Do you enjoy cooking? Is it a chore or a delight? What kind of food do you most enjoy cooking?

9. What patterns have you noticed about your eating?

10. How is food connected to your spirituality?

◎ **READINGS**

Geneen Roth's books
M. F. K. Fisher's books
Overeaters Anonymous literature
Fat Is a Feminist Issue, by Susie Orbach

Hunger Pains, by Mary Pipher, Ph.D.
Live Large! by Cheri Erdman

SUGGESTED ACTIVITIES

1. Bring in your favorite dish to share or your favorite comfort food.

2. Bring in your version of a "quivering green-and-pink molded salad."

3. Bring copies of your favorite recipe.

4. Make a feast together, and then serve it to one another or to guests.

5. Devote an evening to baking bread or making pasta together.

6. Cut out magazine photos, and make a collage of pretty food.

7. Share some of the horror stories of how you have abused food.

8. Tell stories about favorite and worst meals (those termites Sally ate in Guinea)!

9. Bring in the junk food you want to let go of.

10. Fantasize your ideal restaurant, menu, decor, and service.

11. Make a bonfire, and celebrate burning all your diet books!

ALTAR CRAFT

Bring in your favorite pan or kitchen implement. Share about it lovingly as you place it on the altar. Make the meal your centerpiece. Make a display of all the ingredients in a certain recipe. Bring in your favorite cookbook.

> *In search of my mother's garden, I found my own.*
>
> ....
>
> ALICE WALKER
> *In Search of My Mother's Garden*

Our Mothers, Ourselves

If, like so many, your mothering was incomplete and your nurturing instinct underdeveloped, it is time to begin the task of creative healing. Our mother lack is a wound that happens by degrees: some are totally deprived and others only slightly hurt. But for all, the healing

*process involves becoming your own mother—really
caring for yourself, recognizing and filling
your own needs.*

GABRIELLE ROTH,
Maps to Ecstasy

Our relationships with our mothers are the central relationships in our lives, and often they are also the source of great challenge and pain. We may watch ourselves becoming more and more like our mothers as we grow older. Venturing into this core relationship can help bring healing and can heighten our awareness about who we are becoming.

Many possible avenues can be followed as we explore together the theme of relationships with mothers. We might look at our mothers as our first mirrors of ourselves. What they reflected back to us about ourselves we often took as the truth. When we begin to see our mothers as real people, not just as parents, who are struggling as imperfectly as the rest of us to make the journey, we see that what they mirrored back to us about ourselves as children was probably not about us at all but rather about who they were at that time. Talking about our mothers and how we feel about the people they were and are helps us to differentiate ourselves from them, even as we honor our connection with them.

Another interesting approach is to look at what our mothers taught us about nurturing ourselves and others. Many of us grew up with mothers who taught us that while it is noble to take care of others, it is selfish and shameful to take care of oneself. We learned caretaking and codependence rather than self-care and respectful interdependence.

In our circle, there are two mother-daughter groups, including one mother with two daughters. Their honest, respectful sharing on this subject teaches us all. We probably have enough material for a year's worth of meetings on our mothers. You will, too. The challenge is to find a healing balance in this primary relationship. In order to do this, we have to move through some of the darker aspects of our relationships with our mothers. We recommend revisiting this topic over the years.

I . . . have another cup of coffee with my mother. We get along very well, veterans of a guerrilla war we never understood.

. . . .

JOAN DIDION

Slouching Towards Bethlehem

139

◎   GUIDING QUESTIONS

1. What was your relationship with your mother like when you were a child?

2. How about your relationship with your mother as an adult?

3. How do you see your mother's traits and characteristics showing up in you? In your relationships? How do you feel about these similarities?

4. How do you see your mother's traits and characteristics showing up in how you mother? How do you feel about this?

5. What do you most value about your mother?

6. What do you most struggle with about your mother?

◎   READINGS

My Mother / My Self, by Nancy Friday
Revolution from Within, by Gloria Steinem
Women's Bodies, Women's Wisdom, by Christiane Northrup, M.D.
Fruitful: A Real Mother in the Modern World, by Anne Roiphe

◎   SUGGESTED ACTIVITIES

1. Draw a picture of you and your mother when you were a child. Share about it.

2. Draw a picture of your feelings about this relationship. Share about it.

3. Lead people on a guided fantasy about a perfect day with their mother. This day could take place either in current time or at a certain age in the past. What would you have for breakfast, what would you talk about, what would you do, how would you feel? Write or just visualize this perfect day with your mother. Is there anything you could do to bring this nurturing into your life now, either with your mother or just with yourself?

4. Do a journaling exercise in which you ask people to write down, in no particular order or logic, everything they wish

they had received from their mothers. The list might also include what they received that they wish they hadn't. Share these lists with the group. Then ask each person to take the list of what she wanted to receive and consider that this is the list of what she needs to do to nurture herself. (This came from *Revolution from Within*, by Gloria Steinem.)

5. Show a clip from a video of a mother and daughter, for example, Shirley MacLaine and Debra Winger in *Terms of Endearment*.

6. Play a song about mothers, perhaps at the beginning of the meeting. We love the song "Place in My Heart," by Sounds of Blackness.

◎ **ALTAR CRAFT**

Swirl a soft cloth in the center of the circle. Have people bring in pictures of their mothers or of them with their mothers, and arrange the photos on the cloth. Arrange a *matrioshka* doll, the Russian doll where women are nested inside one another. Bring in symbols of maternity (pictures of mother animals, aprons, a warm bowl of custard).

Beauty: Mirror, Mirror on the Wall

While women by the millions have had breast implants, exactly
one man has had experimental surgery to lengthen his penis;
he made the talk shows, which is how I know. And remember
Rogaine? It turns out that this "cure" for baldness—which
supposedly worries and embarrasses men as a visible sign
of aging—didn't go over too well with men: it required
too much effort, cost too much and didn't work very well.
The manufacturers are now shifting their target
market to women with "thin hair."

KATHA POLLIT,
Reasonable Creatures: Essays on Women and Feminism

There could hardly be a hotter topic for a group of women than beauty. Most of us are obsessed with how we look and how far we deviate from how we think we would like to look. Addicted to perfection, we have become merciless self-critics. We have heard a million times the old adage that "beauty is only skin deep," but we have never really internalized it. Instead, we believe that our self-worth is directly correlated to our waist size or the amount of cellulite in our saddlebags. What other adages and myths concerning beauty are we under the spell of?

It can be very liberating to hear other women share their obsessions, thoughts, and feelings about beauty. We begin to hear ourselves in others—others we *know* to be perfectly beautiful. Only then do we see a glimmer of the absurdity of our self-delusions. Bettie is our bona fide college beauty queen—Hopkinsville, Kentucky, 1952. To hear this still-gorgeous sixty-plus-year-old woman describe her negative feelings about her body is to see the real insanity of the obsession. Listening to her discuss this unwinnable dilemma of never-thin-enough, never-young-enough, never-(place your favorite self-recrimination here)-enough makes us all want to wriggle free of our old skins—too tight now, too made up, too coifed—and enjoy the gift of who we really are. Truly, there is no ugliness in a circle of happy women, especially when lit by candles!

What about the taboo topic—competition among women? Given that our cultural identities are so defined by our looks, we naturally compete against other women for men, jobs, money, opportunity, or simply the unspeakable power of being the best-looking woman at the party. If you really want to open up a can of worms, and we usually do, introduce this issue!

*Why not be one's self?
That is the whole
secret of successful
appearance. If one
is a greyhound, why
try to look like
a Pekinese?*

DAME EDITH SITWELL

 GUIDING QUESTIONS

1. Do you think of yourself as beautiful?

2. How has your definition of beauty evolved over the years? Do you feel that you are growing more or less beautiful?

3. How does beauty relate to spirituality?

4. When do you feel most beautiful or most ugly?

5. What do men/women find beautiful?

6. How important is beauty to you?

7. What are your feelings about competing with other women in regard to looks?

8. Have you ever done things to beat out another woman in the looks competition? What did you do? Why? How did you feel afterward?

9. How do you think "lookism" affects your life?

READINGS

The Beauty Myth, by Naomi Wolf
The Cinderella Complex, by Colette Dowling
Fat Is a Feminist Issue, by Susie Orbach

SUGGESTED ACTIVITIES

1. Give one another facials or pedicures or manicures.

2. Stage an inner beauty pageant.

3. Bring in your favorite beauty implement for a show-and-tell.

4. Conduct the "Blessing Way" ritual described in chapter 7.

5. Ask women to come wearing no makeup, and share how that feels.

6. Develop a guided meditation where women see themselves as beautiful as they could possibly imagine themselves being. What would that look like?

7. Ask each woman to bring in a mirror she loves.

8. Talk about some of the myths about beauty.

9. Take Polaroid photos of one another.

10. Draw your body—what you like and don't like about yourself.

11. Have a whole evening on just hair!

12. Play Annie Lennox's "Keep Young and Beautiful" on her *Medusa* CD. Its sarcasm hits the nail right on the beauty mark.

If I did not wear torn pants, orthopedic shoes, frantic disheveled hair, that is to say, if I did not tone down my beauty, people would go mad. Married men would run amuck.

. . . .
BRENDA UELAND

Strength to Your Sword Arm

Arrange in the center of the circle all the beauty implements or mirrors women have brought. This doesn't need to be a solemn altar. Razors and rollers may well find themselves next to an antique perfume bottle. Have photographs of beautiful women from different ages and cultures. Use sweet-smelling candles or diffuse essential oils. Alternately, you could devote your altar to inner beauty. People could bring objects that symbolize aspects of their own inner beauty, such as a big heart, to adorn the altar.

New Paths to Power

An empowered person has gone through the effort to find his or her own truth and is consistently over time living his or her life based on this truth.

DAVID GERSHON AND GAIL STRAUB,
Empowerment: The Art of Creating Your Life As You Want It

The word *power* conjures up a whole range of associations. It's a theme that you will touch on in many different ways throughout your group discussions. Devoting an evening specifically to looking at what power means to each person will reveal the myriad ways that this word speaks to us. The dictionary definition of power is the "ability to do or act; capability of doing or accomplishing something." So power has to do with getting things done, fulfilling one's potential, manifesting or making real one's vision. The power to accomplish is a "doing" form of power. We produce results in external reality, in the external world.

The domain of powerful doing is one in which men have traditionally seemed more competent. Of course, they have also had the resources and the privileges to promote, if not guarantee, their success. The system has valued this kind of power. It's also the power that derives from hierarchy. The rabbi in the synagogue, the principal of the school, the president of the bank, the CEO of a company have, until the last ten

You have no idea how much it costs to make a person look this cheap.

DOLLY PARTON

144

or fifteen years, been men. We women have been socialized to take care of our accomplished husbands and bosses. Both Robin's and Sally's mothers had no jobs outside the home when they were raising small children. If raising children isn't an accomplishment, what is? Yet neither of us grew up believing that our mothers were powerful "doers" because of the way we were conditioned to perceive what is worth doing.

Equally important to us is the "being" kind of power. For those of us who have a sense of what inner or intrinsic power looks like, this form of power is just as easy to detect as the "doing" variety. It may not involve making tons of money or running a big business. Rather, it might take the form of a woman who has developed the inner strength and clarity that allow her to trust her intuition. She has an internal guidance system that is not based solely on meeting others' needs and expectations. She has achieved a kind of mastery over her mental and emotional states. This doesn't mean that she doesn't sometimes think weird thoughts or have occasional "meltdowns." She's not a saint. But she has learned through the practice of self-observation to detect when she is in the throes of negative, self-critical thinking, and, moreover, she knows how to move through these states quickly and constructively.

Our women's group is learning a lot about trusting our intuition and developing intention, being authentic and holding our power. In *The Artist's Way,* Julia Cameron writes,

> The first rule of magic is self-containment. You must hold your intention within yourself, stoking it with power. Only then will you be able to manifest what you desire.

We were deeply affected when we read this. We realized that we had been downright promiscuous in talking about our book with people who weren't exactly thrilled that we were writing it. We had both felt a sort of leaking away of our power, and Cameron's words helped us to identify the problem. It wasn't necessarily that other women were jealous of us—some of them certainly were—but rather that we had unthinkingly exposed ourselves to those who didn't have our best interests at heart.

As awakening women who are reclaiming the power that we have given away or have never even experienced in the

I love people who harness themselves, an ox to a heavy cart, Who pull like water buffalo, with massive patience . . .

....

MARGE PIERCY

145

first place, we desperately need to explore our powers of "being" and "doing." There is no finer vehicle for doing this work than in a supportive community of women.

GUIDING QUESTIONS

1. What do you first think of when you hear the word *power*?
2. Do you think of yourself as powerful?
3. How would you describe your sense of power?
4. When do you feel most powerful? What are you doing when you feel this way?
5. Who is the most powerful person you know? Why? How do you feel when you are around him or her?
6. How has your definition of power changed as you have grown older and wiser?
7. What are your core negative beliefs about your ability to be powerful?
8. How do you sabotage your own sense of power?
9. With whom do you feel most powerful?
10. Do you relate your personal sense of power to a higher power?
11. In which realms do you feel most powerful?
12. How successful have you been at translating your visions into reality?
13. Do you think you are more powerful in the domain of "being" or "doing"? How are they interconnected in your life?

READINGS

Empowerment: The Art of Creating Your Life As You Want It, by David Gershon and Gail Straub

Dreaming the Dark: Magic, Sex and Politics, by Starhawk

The Artist's Way, by Julia Cameron

Enough Is Enough: Exploding the Myth of Having It All, by Carol Orsborne

The Empowered Manager, by Peter Block
Awakening Intuition, by Frances Vaughan

◎ SUGGESTED ACTIVITIES

1. Create a guided meditation where you experience having power in your body, then draw your body with different colors and speak about your drawings.

2. Tell stories about times when you have felt powerless and times when you have felt most powerful.

3. Come dressed in the clothes you feel the most powerful wearing.

4. Write a few wise sentences about power on a piece of paper, fold them up, and put them in a bowl. Then everyone take turns asking a question relating to herself and power. Draw a random response from the bowl. Silently meditate on the relevance and wisdom of the statement.

5. Make up a fantasy about what you would do if you were the most powerful person in the world. Write this in your journal and share with the group.

6. Bring in old magazines, cut out pictures and words, and make a collage of power for yourself or for the group altogether.

7. Do a dance or movement that isolates each area of the body and lets that part lead. Notice which parts of the body feel most powerful and which feel weakest. Discuss.

◎ ALTAR CRAFT

Make a collage of symbols of power ahead of time, and place it in the center of the room surrounded by candles. Have everyone bring in an object that symbolizes power for them. Place these together in the center, and have everyone share about the object as she places it on the altar.

I want us to feel not only our power, but the absolute necessity of using it to the fullest.

. . . .

PATRICIA IRELAND

What Women Want

Giving Birth

Imagine what might happen if the majority of women emerged from their labor beds with a renewed sense of the strength and power of their bodies, and of their capacity for ecstasy through giving birth. When enough women realize that birth is a time of great opportunity to get in touch with their true power, and when they are willing to assume responsibility for this, we will reclaim the power of birth and help move technology where it belongs—in the service of birthing women, not their master.

CHRISTIANE NORTHRUP, M.D.,
Women's Bodies, Women's Wisdom

Giving birth can be a deep and rich topic, even for those who haven't yet or won't ever give birth physically. Everyone of us births things in our lives—ideas, works of art, projects, companies, books, and stories. The process of bringing something from conception to manifestation is birthing, an act for which we women are uniquely equipped.

Like many other aspects of our animal nature, giving birth to children has been medicalized right out of our hands. Most of us boomers were born to mothers who don't remember a thing about our births because they weren't there; they were drugged unconscious. The increase in Caesarean deliveries, induced labors, and other ways of making the process fit the physician's schedule in the last half-century has led to some serious questioning of the way we give birth. Like so much else we've discussed in this book, women are in the process of reclaiming the birthing process as their own, using natural childbirth, birthing rooms, and nurse midwives and even giving birth at home.

It is important to approach this topic very sensitively and respectfully. Strong feelings and attachments to one way of doing things are common. Our group contains a few women who feel strongly about this subject. Robin's sister, Clair, and Jeanne both had home births and are committed to helping other women choose this option. On the other hand, Allison, our labor union leader, just had a very satisfying experience giving birth in a hospital.

Power consists to a large extent in deciding what stories will be told.

CAROLYN HEILBRUN
Writing a Woman's Life

People can feel especially fragile about giving birth because they hate to think that they "did it wrong." We may defend one way of doing it because it's too threatening to think that there might have been a better alternative to the way we gave birth. What might the effects have been on us or our children? So, again, go gently, and avoid the impulse to polarize or convert. Encourage each person to speak of her own experience in "I" statements, and make as much room as you can for the full diversity of views to be voiced.

GUIDING QUESTIONS

1. Describe your birth (physical or symbolic) experience(s). Tell a birth story, a story of when you brought something or someone to life. How are you different because of this?

2. How has birthing affected the rest of your life?

3. What is gestating in you at this time?

4. When you were pregnant, how did you feel?

5. Have you ever had an abortion? How do you feel about that?

6. How does it feel to decide not to have any children in this society?

7. How has it felt to be unable to conceive?

READINGS

The American Way of Birth, by Jessica Mitford
Immaculate Deception I & II, by Suzanne Arms
Reclaiming Our Health, by John Robbins

SUGGESTED ACTIVITIES

1. If one of the members of your group videotaped her birth experience and is comfortable sharing it, show the video as the intro to the meeting. You can also rent or borrow birth videos from any woman-oriented obstetrics office.

2. Give everyone a hunk of clay, and have her sculpt what is gestating in her, what she is about to give

Before I had children I always wondered whether their births would be, for me, like the ultimate in gym class failures. And I discovered instead . . . that I'd finally found my sport.

JOYCE MAYNARD

in *Hers,* edited by
Nancy Newhouse

149

birth to, or what she is currently birthing. Share about the sculpture.

3. Put on some music without any words, and guide people in moving their bodies through the various stages of giving birth—conception, a growing idea or fetus, labor, and delivery. Give people lots of room to interpret this experience as they will. Share about the movement experience with the group.

◎ ALTAR CRAFT

Bring for the altar anything bursting—ripe fruit, round objects, orbs, moons, Venus of Willendorf, pictures of Mother Earth, shells, angels.

Themes for Long-Term Groups

Menstruation: The Bleeding Time

*A big part of healing the planet is related to women regaining
their voice in relationship with their body. The honoring of the
matter of this planet and the female body go hand-in-hand.
We see that ensouling our flow is equivalent to recognizing
the spirit of this earth in all our ecological endeavors. . . .
White antiseptic, bandages like disposable menstrual pads are
the manifestation of menstrual shame and embarrassment.
We are taught to hide them and bury them and keep
secret our flow. It is in this fashion that we
initiate our daughters into womanhood.*

TAMARA SLAYTON, *Reclaiming the Menstrual Matrix*

In preparing to write this piece on menstruation, we consulted our wise, fine friend and group member, Jeanne, who is a real menstrual expert. She observed that menstruation is the most "womanly" of all experiences. All women menstruate or have menstruated. Most of us, however, have never had the opportunity to honestly explore with other women this most "womanly" of subjects, much less listen to others share about it.

Our group devoted two entire sessions to the subject and easily could have done more. In the first session we focused on the onset of menses, and in the second on our current experience of menstruation (or, for those in menopause, their adult experience with menstruation). In both, we found ourselves in fascinating and poignant discussions about the way our society views menstruation and how we have internalized those views.

We can look at the rhythm of the monthly cycle and notice how that rhythm emerges in the rest of our life. For example, ovulation is not only a physical time of fertility, it also can be a natural opportunity for creativity and outwardness in our life psychologically, spiritually, and emotionally. The time when the egg is ready to be fertilized can be opportune for hatching new ideas or projects. It's a time of relating, mating, and interacting.

Likewise, the time just prior to and during menses tends to be a more inward time. Native American traditions allowed women to withdraw physically from the tribe during this time because it was seen as an opportunity for women to receive dreams, visions, and intuitions of both personal and collective significance. Cultures still exist that revere menstruation as an opportunity for spiritual transformation arriving fortuitously every single month. Quite a contrast to our own, which pushes us to deodorize, deny, and hide our blood!

Given the sensitivity of menstruation and the feelings it may engender, we recommend that you wait at least six months, and until there is a high level of trust, before diving into this engrossing realm. The topic of menstruation can elicit lots of issues around body image, sexual abuse, sexuality, and shame. All the more reason to delve in, but do it gently and respectfully.

Our group includes a few women who have given this subject lots of thought and have made many conscious changes in their lives aimed at putting them in deeper relationship with their own menstrual cycles. A few use washable menstrual pads. Others had never given the issue any thought at all. Not surprisingly, people tend to be rather attached to the way they

We need a God that bleeds now. Whose wounds are not the end of anything.

· · · · · · · · ·

NTOZAKE SHANGE

handle their periods, even if they haven't thought about it much. If we had not proceeded sensitively and respectfully, menstrual accouterment could have been a polarizing point for our group. Instead, it was a wonderful opportunity for everyone to share her experience and practices without any single way being considered right.

GUIDING QUESTIONS

1. What was your first period like? Include all the circumstances, feelings, situations, and so forth, that you can remember. How prepared were you? By whom?

2. What is your general experience of your periods currently? Are they heavy or light? What physical symptoms do you experience? What happens emotionally?

3. How do you feel about "that time of the month"? How does it fit into your life? Into your work life? Into your family life? How does it fit into this culture?

4. How healthy do you feel during your premenstrual and menstrual times? What are your habits and practices? Do you have food cravings?

5. Do you notice any correlation between the rhythm of your menstrual cycle and other rhythms in your life? What are they?

6. What are your worst fears about your period?

READINGS

Women's Bodies, Women's Wisdom, by Christiane Northrup, M.D.
Herbal Healing, by Rosemary Gladstone
Hygieia, by Jeannine Parvati
Reclaiming the Menstrual Matrix, Evolving Feminine Wisdom, 2d
    edition, by Tamara Slayton

SUGGESTED ACTIVITIES

1. Create a guided visualization about an ideal first period. Include how you were prepared, the circumstances surrounding it, the

way you felt about it, the way others responded, even a
celebration or rite of passage with your mother and her friends.

2. Plan a guided visualization of the feelings of menstruation—
what the body is doing, what the mind is doing, what the
emotions are up to, what is happening physiologically.

3. Create a guided visualization of living in a culture where
menstruation is not considered nasty or unclean, where it is
valued as a natural part of life. How would life be different?
How would *your* life be different?

4. Have each person draw her experience of menstruation.
Provide paper and lots of colors. Each person can then share
her drawing.

5. Design and conduct a ritual that honors the bleeding time each
month. Ask each person to imagine what she is shedding
symbolically each month and to throw a token piece of red fruit,
a berry, or a piece of red cloth onto a pile in the center of the
room. Then, each person can take a sip of red juice and say what
it symbolizes, some way that she needs nourishment, something
she needs in her life to keep her (figurative) womb fertile.

6. Everyone wear red.

◉ **ALTAR CRAFT**

Decorate the center of the circle with a red cloth swirled in a
circle. Place on it a moon bowl (this is a bowl for soaking
washable menstrual pads). Bring red fruit, perhaps a
pomegranate, raspberries, apples, or goblets of cranberry or
cherry juice. Add menstrual accoutrement, any and all types.

Money: Making It and Spending It

*Do you focus your mental awareness on abundance and
prosperity—or do you place it on lack and limitation?*

DAVID GERSHON AND GAIL STRAUB,
Empowerment: The Art of Creating Your Life as You Want It

We don't know anyone, male or female, who has a simple, straight-forward relationship with money. All of us learned attitudes about money early on from our families. Sally's family, for instance, seemed secure in every way except financially. Neither of her parents had much skill or interest in the arena of domestic finance, and neither earned much money. Polite conversation never included the topic of money, so one never asked how much Daddy earned, even though one was dying to know. So Sally grew up with certain notions and implied values about money: It's not nice to talk about or even care very much about money; it's hard and complicated to balance a checkbook; there's never enough money; even if there were enough, it's not seemly to spend it in flashy ways.

In Robin's family, a different dynamic was at work. Money was synonymous with power, and both the power and the purse strings were under the control of her father. Her mother was to take care of her children and husband, while Daddy would take care of the rest. Money was used to motivate, reward, and punish. The clear and unstated implication of this arrangement was that supporting the family financially was the higher and more significant calling, and the bottom line was, it's Dad's money, so he gets his way.

In many of our families, men were the breadwinners and women spent their money, unless, of course, they did something to irritate the man. Then they would feel the financial reins tighten just a bit around their necks. Others of us had mothers who worked hard at low-paying jobs to make ends meet. Few of us had role models of women who were either financially independent or who felt confident in such matters. As a consequence, many of us have remained childlike and dependent in our attitudes, even if we are supporting ourselves.

A friend of Sally's in her late sixties, who considers herself liberated and a feminist, just spent a thousand dollars on clothes in a New York boutique. She confessed that she paid for half of it in cash and put the other half on a credit card so as to fly below her husband's financial radar screen. Sound familiar? How many times have we sneaked purchases into the house? Or, how many of us are addicted to spending money or are drowning in credit card debt?

It's easy to be independent when you have money. But to be independent when you haven't got a thing—that's the Lord's test.

MAHALIA JACKSON

You may wonder what all this has to do with spirituality. After all, God and mammon cannot be worshiped together. And didn't Jesus chase the money lenders out of the temple? Who said what about "filthy lucre"? And isn't money the root of all evil? Why would we ever want to talk about something so crass as money with our special spiritual friends, in our lovely serene circle?

There are plenty of reasons! First of all, we need to start deprogramming ourselves from our negative beliefs and feelings about money. A woman who is walking around with a wallet full of maxed-out credit cards is probably in trouble. She will not be able to feel grateful, she will be feeling desperate. Couple this with an underlying mentality focused on scarcity, which tells us that we can't ever have what we really want. Then add the palpitations and sweaty palms that come every time April 15 looms onto the horizon and we start trying to remember the whereabouts of that shoe box full of receipts. This may be starting to sound like a *Cathy* cartoon, but, we submit, it is an all-too-real picture.

We need to become financially conscious as part of the process of coming into our full spiritual power. A women's spirituality group is an excellent venue for initiating the process of becoming financially empowered. Starting to uncover one's beliefs and feelings about money is a key first step on the way to gaining competence, balance, and clarity.

◎   GUIDING QUESTIONS

1. Start by free-associating with the word *money*.

2. What was your family's economic status?

3. Did your family talk about money freely and openly, or was it a taboo topic?

4. What is "enough" money for you?

5. Do you and your partner share similar values about money?

6. Do you spend more than you earn?

7. Do you save? How?

8. How are finances handled in your home today?

9. Do you have hang-ups about making and spending money?

Money is something we choose to trade our life energy for.

VICKI ROBIN

AND JOE DOMINGUEZ

Your Money or Your Life

155

10. How much of your time do you spend thinking about making
or spending money?

◉ READINGS

Empowerment: The Art of Creating Your Life as You Want It, by Gail
Straub and David Gershon
Your Money or Your Life, by Vicki Robin and Joe Dominguez
Plain and Simple, by Sue Bender
Downshifting: Reinventing Success on a Slower Track, by Amy
Saltzman

◉ SUGGESTED ACTIVITIES

1. Draw a road map of your life to this point, with key personal
economic milestones on it (for example, when you got a raise,
bought a car, filed taxes for the first time, got a social security
card, took your first job).

2. Brainstorm a list of questions that you have about money. Find
out if someone in the group has the expertise to answer any of
them. If so, break into small groups for a little teach-in.

3. Do a guided visualization, imagining what your life would be
like if you were really poor or if you were really rich. What do
the different lifestyles look like? Are there similarities?

4. Make a list of the ways you sabotage yourself financially. Share
the list. Pick one or two ways, and commit to the group to stop
doing them.

5. Talk about the degree to which you feel financially secure.
Share steps you have taken to feel more secure.

6. Do a group meditation: going around in a circle, imagine each
woman fully competent and confident in handling her finances.

7. Make up a lottery. Have someone win a million dollars. Give
her monopoly money. Ask what she would spend it on.

◉ ALTAR CRAFT

(A sense of humor is important here!) Bring in all different
kinds of currency, checkbooks, tax forms, passbook savings

accounts, stock certificates, and so forth. Arrange it all in a big heap in the center of the floor. Or have each woman place something in the middle that indicates how she feels good about her finances. Arrange a collection of your or your children's piggy banks.

Menopause: The Wisdom Years

The change of life is a time of release when a woman begins to reap the benefits of all that she has learned and done. It is the time when her spiritual life at last truly begins. Menopause is a process of rebirth from which a woman emerges with new responsibilities, new mirrors, and new power. At its nucleus is the discovery by each woman of her own personal mystery, an illumination of her private relationship to the totality of her own life processes. As she develops, she begins to choreograph the new energies of the universe in a new way.

LYNNE V. ANDREWS,
Woman at the Edge of Two Worlds: The Spiritual Journey Through Menopause

Even if many or most of the women in the group have not yet undergone menopause, we know that everyone eventually will. It is worthwhile to devote an evening to this topic. The evening can be a combination of inspiration and information sharing. A tremendous amount of fear and misinformation about menopause circulates in our society. Like childbirth, menopause has been medicalized, treated like an illness instead of as a normal development in a woman's life. In Native American cultures, women going through menopause were accorded special respect. After they had finished their thirteenth moon, a lunar year, without a period, they were considered wiser now that they were "holding their blood."

Most women in our culture feel that menopause is something to be gotten over with as quickly and as privately as possible. When, at forty, Sally had her surgical menopause, that is, a hysterectomy (which she is now convinced was totally

Do not deprive me of my age. I have earned it.

MAY SARTON
The Poet and the Donkey

157

unnecessary), she was put immediately on estrogen replacement therapy, so she had only an occasional hot flash. But the gynecologist didn't warn her about the weight gain, the incontinence, the vaginal dryness or painful intercourse. None of these are pleasant occurrences, but they are all totally normal. Maybe once we all start sharing about menopause, we will develop a healthier perspective on this natural process than the medical profession has offered us thus far. At least in our culture. Robin has a friend who is an expert on international women's health who reports that hot flashes and other symptoms of what in our culture is considered an illness (menopause) don't exist in many African cultures. There are virtually no widely suffered medical problems associated with menopause, just as there are not taboos surrounding menstruation and its cessation in these places.

*I can't actually
see myself putting
makeup on my face at
the age of sixty. But I
can see myself going
on a camel train
to Samarkand.*

GLENDA JACKSON

GUIDING QUESTIONS

1. How are you experiencing menopause physically, emotionally, and spiritually?

2. How do you cope with hot flashes, incontinence, vaginal dryness, and so forth?

3. What are your fears about menopause?

4. How did your mother and grandmother experience it?

5. What if men had menopause?

6. What images of menopause are portrayed in the media?

7. What is positive about menopause?

8. What is fertile within you?

9. Do you still feel sexy? If not, how does that feel?

10. Who are your menopausal role models? Why?

READINGS

Women of the Fourteenth Moon, an anthology of readings about menopause, edited by Dena Taylor
Women's Bodies, Women's Wisdom, by Christiane Northrup, M.D.

Getting Over Getting Older, by Letty Cottin Pogrebin
Dr. Susan Love's Hormone Book

◎   **SUGGESTED ACTIVITIES**

1. Create and conduct a croning ritual for the women who have undergone, or are undergoing, menopause. In it, symbolically release menstruation, and claim the power and wisdom that come with growing older. You may want to have each person name what she is releasing and what she is claiming.

2. Work with clay or make pictures. Paint on one another's bodies.

3. Visualize a world where older women are given the highest respect. Then discuss how it would feel to live in that world.

4. Show one another our hysterectomy scars (lumpectomy, mastectomy, too).

5. Make a ritual for surgically confiscated uteruses.

6. Create a collage of images of stronger, wiser older women.

7. Everyone wear purple!

◎   **ALTAR CRAFT**

Make an altar of menstrual products that no longer will be needed, then remove them from the altar one by one during a reading. Fashion tampon candles and menstrual pad flowers. Make a centerpiece of photographs of older women, both relatives and strangers. Add ripe sheaves of wheat or herbal preparations that ease the symptoms of hot flashes. Or, place things on the altar that symbolize the power and wisdom we are entering into in our menopausal years.

Climaxes and Contradictions: Talking About Sex

*Our experience of sex . . . most likely will be internally as well
as externally contradictory. When I talk about sex, and most
particularly when I talk about myself, I am struggling to
be as honest as I can be. But I'm haunted by the fact that
nothing I can say will be complete. . . . Sex is a game, a
weapon, a toy, a joy, a trance, an enlightenment, a loss,
a hope. I contradict myself because nothing I say can
ever be enough. It's all true, though—just about
everything is true. Especially the contradictions.*

SALLY TISDALE,
Talk Dirty to Me

Sex is both the least- and most-talked-about subject in America. It is
in front of our faces constantly, in the media, movies, magazines, books,
and TV. And yet how often do we talk honestly about sex in our own
lives and our own experience rather than about how we or others think
it should be? Not often, which is why we are pretty hung up about it.
The God of our fathers had plenty to say about sexuality. Our bodies
were unclean, and sex was natural only in prescribed circumstances. In a
women's spirituality group we are working toward a more
woman-friendly attitude. Women's spirituality is embodied
spirituality.

Sex is a loaded topic, an especially sensitive theme. Each
of us holds layer upon layer of issues and feelings regarding
sex. Our cultural identities as women are powerfully defined
by our sexiness, whether we like it or not. Then there are issues of sexual abuse. Statistically speaking, in a group of ten
women, at least four will have been victims of sexual abuse.
Many of us don't talk about sex with our very best friend or
even our partners, much less a circle of ten she-probably-
has-a-perfect-sex-life-anyway-so-I-won't-say-what-I-really-
feel women. In our group it was not too surprising that the
night we did this one, lots of people didn't make it, just for-

*Everyone lies about
sex, more or less,
to themselves if not
to others, to others
if not themselves,
exaggerating its
importance or
minimizing its pull.*

DAPHNE MERKIN
Out of the Garden

160

got, or had another more pressing commitment. It's challenging to talk about sex.

Go gently, and trust each person to reveal as much as she is ready to. You may want to focus on one aspect of sexuality, for instance, the initial sexual experience or people's current experience of sex. Or you may want to let the discussion wander as people choose what they want to focus on. If your group has both lesbian and straight women in it, make sure that the discussion is inclusive. Our session included an anatomy lesson and a discussion of the physiology of orgasms. However, the real juice in this topic doesn't live in information, it lives in the sharing of stories and the airing of feelings and fears, beliefs and perceptions. If we speak openly and listen carefully, we just might find we are not as different from others as we usually believe we are.

This was one of the few sessions in which having mothers, daughters, and sisters in the group made it a little more difficult to be candid. Be mindful of these kinds of dynamics. And, given how difficult it is for most people to talk honestly about sex, it would be a good idea to introduce it after the group has a high level of trust and intimacy.

◎   GUIDING QUESTIONS

1. What was your first sexual experience like? Was it hetero or homosexual?

2. What about your first experience of intercourse?

3. What have been your best and worst sexual encounters?

4. How are you currently experiencing sex?

5. How do the media and other cultural expressions influence your feelings about your sexuality?

6. What is your worst fear about sex?

7. What do you like about sex?

8. What is your ideal sexual scene?

9. How has your understanding of your sexual self changed as you've grown older?

READINGS

> *Talk Dirty to Me,* by Sally Tisdale
> *Touching Fire: Erotic Writings by Women,* edited by Louise
>   Thornton, Jan Sturtevant, and Amber Coverdale Sumrall
> *The Delta of Venus,* by Anaïs Nin
> *A New View of a Woman's Body,* Federation of Feminist Women's
>   Health Centers
> *Sexual Happiness for Women: An Illustrated Practical Guide to Sexual
>   Fulfillment,* by Maurice Jaffe and Elizabeth Fenwick

SUGGESTED ACTIVITIES

1. Have one of the leaders prepare a "new" anatomy lesson,
   including placement and function of the major organs and
   tissues connected with orgasm. Use visual aids.

2. Create a guided visualization in which each person can reinvent
   her first sexual experience. Ask lots of questions to help each
   person design the perfect first sexual encounter for herself.
   Share these with one another, if desired.

3. Use the guiding questions as suggested for the visualization, but
   have people write their ideal first sexual experience in a
   journal. Share the writing, or parts of it, with one another.

4. Draw your sexual self with colors and shapes that exude the
   real sexual you.

5. Talk about masturbation.

6. Read erotic passages, and talk about what turns you on.

ALTAR CRAFT

Make a shrine of sensual scarves, lingerie, incense, candles,
sexual toys, vibrators.

Death and Dying

*Intermittency—an impossible lesson for human beings to
learn. How can one learn to live through the ebb tides of one's
existence? How can one learn to take the trough of the wave?
It is easier to understand here on the beach where the
breathlessly still ebb-tides reveal another life below
the level which mortals usually reach. In this
crystalline moment of suspense, one has a
sudden revelation of the secret kingdom
at the bottom of the sea.*

ANNE MORROW LINDBERGH,
Gift from the Sea

We haven't lost anyone in our group yet, but we have felt death's cold
breath on the backs of our necks. We've dealt with Sandra's breast cancer (caught at an early stage) and the cancer of Taylor, Robin's two-year-
old niece. Remarkably little fresh, blunt grief has visited us over these
past four years. Yet we all know that this is but a temporary reprieve.

The challenge is to work with death in a way that illuminates the subject without becoming morbid or saccharine. We need to hear ourselves
talk about death—our own and that of our loved ones. In this way, we
can be present to one another as we prepare ourselves for our death—
what the Tibetans consider to be life's supreme moment. We are not
talking about our imminent deaths, although who really knows? Rather,
our goals are to live fully in the present moment without denying or
fearing the inevitability of death, and to be able to be present to others
as they struggle with dying and loss.

There is likely to be lots of emotion present in a meeting
focused on death and dying. The leaders are responsible for
making the space safe enough for people to express their feelings or just to feel in their own way. Have tissues readily available. Grief will become plain; even losses that we thought we
were long past may unexpectedly surface. Allowing people an
empathetic place to emote is a tremendous gift, the essence of
healing. Be careful not to feel obliged to make it all better. You

*Death, in its way,
comes as just as much
of a surprise as birth.*

....

EDNA O'BRIEN

A Rose in the Heart

163

can't, and it would be wise to remind all the well-meaning, loving hearts in your group of this fact before your plunge into this subject.

Group members may also want to share about the powerful experience of being with a dying person. It is common to have a vivid memory of the last words from a dying person and to have tried to incorporate these words into one's life purpose. Sally's ninety-eight-year-old grandmother, Gertrude, died this past January in a city across the country. Sally had visited her last August. At that time Gertrude recognized that she wasn't going to live much longer, despite her good health, and she made this clear. Rather than denying her impending death and keeping a chin-up attitude, Sally took this to heart and bid her a very emotionally satisfying and clear farewell.

◎ **GUIDING QUESTIONS**

1. Have you ever seen a dead person or been with a dying one? What was that like?

2. What do you think dying is like?

3. What are you most afraid of about death? How does this affect you?

4. How do you protect yourself from thinking about death?

5. What do you think happens after death?

6. What are your beliefs about heaven and hell, reincarnation?

7. What losses are you still grieving?

◎ **READINGS**

On Death and Dying, by Elisabeth Kübler-Ross
The Tibetan Book of Living and Dying, by Sogyal Rinpoche
Who Dies?, by Stephen Levine
How We Die, by Sherwin Nuland
Cries of the Spirit, an anthology of poems and readings, edited by Marilyn Sewell
Being with Dying, by Joan Halifax
Life to Death: Harmonizing the Transition, by Hulen S. Kornfield and Richard W. Boerstler
A Midwife to the Dying Process, by Timothy E. Quill, M.D.

SUGGESTED ACTIVITIES

1. Write a make-believe obituary for yourself. Share obituaries with one another.

2. Share about your ideal memorial service or the funeral arrangements you would like to have made for yourself.

3. Do a guided meditation, and visualize your own death.

4. Share information about living wills and other advance medical directives.

5. Imagine a future incarnation, or share about a past one.

6. Share about taking care of a dying person.

7. Sing a gospel song.

ALTAR CRAFT

Read up on Egyptian funerary arrangements, where people are buried with their favorite objects. Ask people to bring in an object that they would like to have buried with them. Have people share about these objects as they are placing them on the altar. Or, people might bring in pictures of loved ones who have died, making an ancestral shrine as the Vietnamese do.

Themes for Any Group, Anytime

The Seasons: Reconnecting to the Rhythms of the Earth

The earth is my sister; I love her daily grace, her silent daring,
and how loved I am, how we admire this strength in each
other, all that we have lost, all that we have suffered,
all that we know: we are stunned by this beauty, and
I do not forget: what she is to me, what I am to her.

SUSAN GRIFFIN,
Woman and Nature

The seasons are powerful metaphors. As practitioners of women's spirituality, we find meaning and beauty in the seasonal turn. The spring is a time to celebrate new beginnings; in summer we harvest the fruits of our efforts; the fall is a time for letting go and releasing; and in winter we go within to rest, conserve our energy, and replenish our reserves. We can't help wondering what the world would be like if these properties of the seasons were guiding principles for all our activities. It might mean that we wouldn't be trying to run ourselves into a frenzy around the holidays but instead would spend time at home, sleeping more, cocooning, and staying cozy with friends and family.

We like to weave the seasons into almost all our meetings. For example, a recent August meeting was arranged around this time of abundance. The purpose of the evening was to reconnect with one another after summer vacations and to bid farewell to two members who were moving away. The altar held a colorful display of garden produce, harvested minutes before the meeting. And the guiding question was, "What is your summer's harvest?" The session wasn't *about* summer so much as it *was* late summer, warm and brimming with bounty. As usual, each woman shared fully, interpreting the question to suit herself.

Autumn is a good time for cleaning out your closet and getting rid of those size eights you'll never fit into for more than two hours after a starvation diet (and we're not doing those anymore, remember?). Have a clothing swap in which everyone brings in her unwanted clothes and swaps with everyone else. Go home with a new wardrobe for free. See if you can bring out the spiritual side of this swap. How is it like your relationships with one another? Sweep leaves together, make a big pile, and bury yourselves in them. Remember what it felt like to be a kid in the fall. Did you look forward to going back to school, or did you dread it? How does the leaving of the light affect you?

Winter is the inner season. Where are your favorite places and ways to hibernate? Share those with the group. Drink hot chocolate together in front of the fire. Create gifts of the heart for one another. Read poetry by candlelight. Decorate the altar with evergreen boughs. Make up a ritual to celebrate Santa Lucia, the beloved saint/goddess who comes into

> We are of the earth,
> made of the same
> stuff; there is no
> other, no division
> between us and
> "lower" or "higher"
> forms of being.
>
> **ESTELLA LAUDER**
>
> *Women as Mythmakers*

houses wearing a crown of candles. Prepare a celebration for the return of the light.

And spring . . . is this not everyone's favorite season? What is being born within you? Where are the shoots of new growth? Come wearing—what else?—green. Read the poems of Hildegard of Bingen, the twelfth-century abbess, composer, artist, herbalist, and visionary. She wrote about the greening of the world and defined sin as being "dried up." Conduct a planting ritual; actually plant some seeds together and articulate what each seed symbolizes in your life. What do you want to grow? Dye Easter eggs. Make a Passover seder. Create an altar with palm fronds and eggs, daffodils and forsythia.

It's easy to understand how our ancestors found ways to celebrate this seasonal turning. The pagan calendar has eight festivals, the equinoxes and solstices plus the cross-quarter days bisecting the four quarters. We don't follow this calendar in our group, but plenty of books of Wiccan and pagan rituals celebrate these days if you want to go into a little more depth here.

Is there a way to bring the season into your meeting? To bring everyone closer to Gaia? To bring the outside inside? In doing so, whether it is the primary focus of your evening or just a harmonious element blending in the background, you bring yourselves in a little closer touch with the natural rhythms of nature and all she has to teach us.

Potpourris and Pajama Parties

Not all of our meetings are serious, and hardly any of our serious meetings are somber. We love to laugh together, and we almost always do. There are some hilariously funny women in our group. Sandra, in particular, could do stand-up comedy routines that people would pay money to see. Jeanne is a dancer by training and is a great physical comedienne. We think we are all fairly compelling storytellers, with widely diverging interests. Sally, for example, is an avid gardener, studies drumming, organizes events, writes, and pays attention to national and local politics. Robin isn't the slightest bit interested in the current political scene. She'd rather be dancing,

Nature has been for me, for as long as I can remember, a source of solace, inspiration, adventure, and delight; a home, a teacher, a companion.

LORRAINE ANDERSON

Sisters of the Earth

167

or spending time with her husband and son. Sandra is fiercely committed to women's rights, Allison to working people and her husband and three small boys, Jeanne to humane birthing practices, her movement classes, and her kids. One Laura is studying to teach English to foreigners and learning to practice yoga therapy, and the other Laura is a graphic artist and designer. Antoinette teaches a movement alignment technique called the Alexander Method and also teaches science to kids. Sandra and Bettie are consummate, practically professional grandmothers. Susan trains people to mediate and resolve conflicts. So we all have different agendas and priorities.

Sometimes, especially in the summer when our ranks dwindle and no one volunteers to be the mother, we have a potpourri of a group, a kind of show-and-tell of meaningful objects, questions, ideas, and stories—whatever we want to bring in to the group. This gives us the chance to revel in our diversity. These evenings are hardly structured at all, but they develop a cohesive, flowing quality. It's wonderful to lay out these different threads. By the end of the evening, we have woven them all together, and we haven't even been trying. We recommend this kind of a spontaneous evening at least once a year. This is also one of the only times that we recommend giving each person a prespecified time limit for sharing.

We have been dying to have a pajama party where we all sleep over at someone's house, eat junk food, watch movies, play with one another's hair, and generally act like teenagers—where we just have fun and be silly for no good reason except that it is good for our souls. Your group gets bonus points if you can manage to carve out the time in everyone's busy schedules for some kind of play date. Maybe we could even rope some of our more adventurous partners into conducting a panty raid!

Nature doesn't move in a straight line, and as part of nature, neither do we.

....

GLORIA STEINEM

Revolution from Within

Additional Suggestions

These topics are meant to serve as suggestions only. We could just as easily have outlined other themes, like music, a sense of place, friendship, time, home, inspiration, leadership, listening, keeping secrets, movement/dance/body awareness, personal vision, political direct action (going together to a demonstration against domestic violence, making a panel for the AIDS quilt). The possibilities are endless, and even when you repeat a theme, you will find added depth and dimension.

9

Home Remedies to Keep Your Group Healthy

An honorable human relationship—that is, one in which . . .
people have the right to use the word love—is a process,
delicate, violent, often terrifying . . . , a process of refining
truths they can tell each other. It is important to do this
because it breaks down self-delusion and isolation. . . .
It is important to do this because we can count on
so few people to go that hard way with us.

ADRIENNE RICH

*G*rowing spiritually entails learning
to be in loving relationship with one another—learning to walk that delicate balance beam of being truly ourselves and accepting others as who they are. It means being honest even when someone may be hurt. It means asking hard questions. It means finding out how we affect other people. It means questioning our assumptions about what is right and wrong, and who is right and wrong. This kind of growing requires committed relationships, because if you don't have that, people will bolt when things get messy. This chapter is about how a group of human

beings can develop and maintain healthy committed relationships that "have the right to use the word love."

As with any organic system, your group will definitely experience ebbs and flows of its energy over time. Just because you have all signed on "till death do you part" (or for a year or six months) does not mean that every group meeting will be scintillating and every topic one that you are just dying to delve into. The first meeting or two can be like love at first sight; everyone may be madly excited about everyone else. But as in any other relationship, once the honeymoon is over and the hormones die down, people will start getting on one another's nerves. This does not mean that divorce is imminent, just that it's time for a little work on the relationship. By the way, some of the best groups start slowly and build toward greater intimacy. Whichever way your group grows, it will take consciousness and courage from everyone to foster intimacy and cohesion.

It will also take awareness on the part of everyone to keep your group healthy. What do we mean by a healthy group? The definition we propose is this: **A healthy group is one that nurtures the growth of all of its members.** The two key points are *growth* and *inclusion*. The group must work for all of the members, not just for some of them. By growth, we mean spiritual growth, very broadly defined. We return here to the idea of "containers of emergence"; inclusion involves creating a group environment that is spacious enough to hold everyone. When a group is inclusive and there is a sense of belonging, then women feel safe to emerge as individuals.

The key to a powerful group is the quality of the relationships. We have all seen (or been in) bad but long-lasting marriages. In a spirituality group we are aiming instead for healthy relationships that can last over the period of time chosen by group members. The key to healthy and long-lasting groups is practicing the Circle Basics: rotating leadership, practicing council sharing, listening without an agenda, and taking responsibility for one's own needs. When all is said and done, these practices are the best medicine for group health. This chapter offers additional practical advice on keeping your group fit throughout its time together, whether that is six months or six years. If you've been meeting for a while, this chapter will be useful in identifying and addressing any issues that have emerged thus far. If you are just beginning your group, we recommend that you revisit this chapter within the next year.

We have put this chapter here, near the end, to encourage you to go deeper even when the going isn't so smooth. It is there, beyond the politeness, that many real spiritual lessons are learned. But we can go there only if we are willing to sacrifice looking good and let ourselves surrender to the ride.

Stages of Group Development

As with any living system, your group will change over time. This is natural, normal, and actually desirable. We all know this in the back of our minds, yet it is amazing how often we still enter groups (or romantic involvements or friendships) with the expectation that we will enjoy instant bliss and total intimacy, with none of the mess! Let us remind you gently, one of the few guarantees we can give you is that *this won't happen.* Your group will probably go through various stages on your way to building strength and inclusiveness. Being aware of these stages can help you in moving through them gracefully.

As group facilitators, we have studied and practiced many of the group dynamics theories, and the best description of the stages of group development that we know comes from Scott Peck in his book *The Different Drum: Community Making and Peace.* We like his theory because Peck draws his principles not only from his formal education as a psychiatrist but also from his direct experience in community building. Peck works intentionally with groups to transform them into communities. He has worked with hundreds of diverse groups, ranging in size from twelve to four hundred people each, and he has made some simple yet profound observations about what it takes to become emotionally and spiritually bonded.

Stage One: Pseudocommunity

The first stage of community, according to Peck, is called pseudocommunity. This is the initial phase of getting to know

Nothing important was ever accomplished without courage and risk. In fact, that's one true criterion for all effective thinking and action now: does it take courage? Does it seem incredibly risky on many fronts—to my personal life? my professional life? Other useful questions are: Will I be laughed at? Will I be misunderstood? Does it require that I trust my feelings? Does it require that I use faculties that have lain dormant for the most part in humans for millennia: spirit, intuition, imagination, independence of judgment, love of women? If so it is very promisingly "womanly," and therefore powerful and I should seriously consider it.

SONIA JOHNSON
Out of Our Minds

one another. He calls this "pseudo" because, although it may feel warm and fuzzy, it's not real, for it is based on superficial interactions, not true intimacy. The tendency at the beginning is for people to be very cordial and charming to one another. We put our best feet forward. We look like we have it all together, or at least we try very hard to create this impression. We want people to like us, and we want to be comfortable. So we are very nice and pleasant. But "beware of instant community," Peck warns. When we believe that we have bonded very quickly, without any muss or fuss, we are kidding ourselves.

While this is a natural stage of development, it is an early one, an immature one. Missing is true intimacy and an atmosphere of deep acceptance. Differences between people are underplayed, even denied. There is no significant self-disclosure. Many communities, even churches and synagogues, have gotten stuck in pseudocommunity. "Genuine communities may experience lovely and sometimes lengthy periods free from conflict. But that is because they have learned how to deal with conflict rather than avoid it," says Peck. "Pseudocommunity is conflict-avoiding; true community is conflict-resolving."

Stage Two: Chaos

The second stage of group development is chaos. Sound appealing? Well, if you haven't been there yet, you will pass through this country on the way to true community. In this phase, the white gloves come off, and differences between people surface. No longer will the group tolerate one member making blanket statements that apply to everyone. For instance, when Judy remarks, "We all know it is important to bring our children up in the church to gain a sense of tradition," instead of being met with a polite silence, as in pseudocommunity, someone will speak up and say, "*You* may think so, but *I* don't. I wouldn't let my kids near a church."

In stage two, not only are the differences in opinions, views, attitudes, and feelings put on the table, the differences are the main event. This is a stage of struggle and fighting. Usually, we are so uncomfortable with other people viewing

Once conform, once do what other people do because they do it, and a lethargy steals over all the finer nerves and faculties of the soul.

VIRGINIA WOOLF

The Common Reader

life differently that we make it our mission to change them. We assume they must be fixed, and we go about it ardently. The discussions will sound like battles of will, and they are. This is a power struggle: Who is right? Who will prevail?

Now, it is hard to imagine a group of well-mannered ladies going at it like this. Struggle for power is behavior we usually attribute to men, but it takes place, perhaps with some variation, among women as well. Conflict arises, and we try our best to obliterate it by "setting those people straight." The conflict is nasty only because we label it so due to our discomfort with it. Conflict is necessary and healthy, like the terrible twos. You hope and pray your kid won't be a toddler forever, but something would be amiss if she skipped that stage entirely.

In the rush to get through this stage, groups often choose one very common, but illusory, escape route. Many groups will try to create a structure or policies, thinking these will eliminate the issues aroused in chaos. They will make rules, trying to prevent chaos and conflict from occurring. Sometimes this structure is appropriate, but often it is an attempt to control something that is, by definition, not to be controlled. Chaos is to be waded through, not straitjacketed. So be aware of this tendency to regulate chaos out of existence, and ask yourselves what may be underlying your sudden need for structure and rules.

Usually what helps a group move on from this stage is for someone to have the guts to reflect the group's actions back to itself. "Seems like we went from being super-nice to being consumed by trying to change one another." Just a simple observation, without evaluation or judgment, may awaken the group's self-awareness enough to move it into the next phase. Or it may take a few more rounds in the ring before the group moves on.

Stage Three: Emptiness

Peck calls the third stage of becoming a community "emptiness." In some ways, this can be the most challenging and crucial phase of all because "it is the bridge between chaos and

There can be no reconciliation where there is no open warfare. There must be a battle, with pennants waving and cannons roaring, before there can be peaceful treaties and enthusiastic shaking of hands.

MARY ELIZABETH BRADDON

Lady Audley's Secret

community." The fact that this phase sounds mystical is no mistake. This stage consists of emptying ourselves of the ideas, beliefs, attitudes, and assumptions that make us impervious to really hearing another person. Another way of describing this phase is that it is a way of clearing away psychological blocks so that our spiritual selves can flourish.

Here's an example. Maria, forty-five, a divorced working woman and single parent, adopted an attitude, without even realizing it, about Denise, an attractive fiftyish woman who is immaculately groomed and elegantly dressed and who lives in the chichi part of town. Everything Denise says, Maria questions. She sees Denise as superficial, privileged, and out of touch with the real world of working women and their problems. Not really trusting Denise, Maria subtly keeps her distance. Since she is blocked from Denise by her largely unconscious attitudes, her chances of deepening a relationship with Denise are low to nonexistent.

During the emptiness stage, the key question each person needs to ask is: What stands in my way of communicating with the people in this group? Can I let these things go? For Maria, her attitude toward Denise stands in the way of real communication. Denise's makeup, hair, and general demeanor remind Maria of her ex-husband's family and friends. She was convinced they thought they were better than she was, and so she always felt insecure and inadequate around them. To deal with this, Maria decided they were all snobs and began to look down on them. Maria has extended this whole set of beliefs and attitudes to Denise without even realizing it. To be in true community with Denise, she will need to empty herself of these beliefs. Then, and only then, can she really get to know Denise.

Peck identifies several types of blocks that most people will need to recognize and rid themselves of in the emptiness stage.

Expectations and preconceptions keep us living in the "what if" instead of the "what is." Instead of really experiencing what the group is offering us, we are busy trying to mold the group into our idea of what it should be offering us.

There is no birth of consciousness without pain.

....

CARL JUNG

Prejudices arise when we typecast people into premade roles. The story about Maria and Denise is an example of prejudice. It takes time for individuals to bring to the conscious realm the prejudices they hold about one another, and then even more time to be able to let them go.

Ideology, theology, and solutions are some of the ways we try to convince one another to see "the right way," which in every case just happens (surprise!) to be our way. In emptying ourselves, we don't necessarily relinquish our own belief systems, but we *are* asked to let go of the conviction that there is just one way to see reality.

The need to heal, convert, fix, or solve comes into play when we believe we are acting out of the goodness of our hearts and want to help. We see someone with a problem we have been through, and our natural tendency is to explain how we solved it for ourselves. But even though we think we are being loving, usually the need to heal, convert, fix, or solve comes from the need to make ourselves feel better. We are uncomfortable with the pain someone else is experiencing, maybe because it hits a raw nerve in us. We want to quell the anguish, so we step in as healer and helper.

The need to control is not too hard to figure out. We may have a strong need for members in the group to behave a certain way with one another, perhaps always kind and gentle or always "spiritual" in some lofty sense. In order to accomplish this goal, we try to control. We unconsciously maneuver the group to avoid what is not on our agenda. For example, if Robin started the group and it appears to be in chaos, with people struggling all around her, she is probably going to experience some fear. She will say to herself, "People are going to quit. They are going to blame me if they don't have a good time. I better make sure that we start being nice to one another, whatever it takes." It's very hard, especially for leaders, to let a group find its way through these stages and not step in to nudge it, out of fear, in a particular direction. Emptying oneself of the need to control allows the group to come through on its own strength and in its own way.

These are not easy habits to surrender. Often, the things we need to give up to create community are just the things that have tripped us up in relationships countless times before. And that is precisely one of the ways in which sacred community is a spiritual path. It presents us, over and over again, with the challenge to become conscious of what separates us from Spirit.

Maria's prejudice toward Denise is really based on an underlying belief that she herself is inadequate. And it so happens that wealthy, educated people trigger that belief in her. By bringing it to consciousness, owning the belief as her own, and emptying herself of it, she can reset her beliefs about who she really is. She will have earned the right to affirm, "I, Maria, am a divine being, lovable and totally adequate. This adequacy and lovableness have nothing to do with my education, my wealth, my worldly success. I was born with it." Emptiness is a profound experience of growth. As difficult as it is to move through, it is the only route to true, mature community.

Emptiness is the stage in which we let down our guard with one another. As Peck puts it, "community requires the confession of brokenness." That is, we use all the energy that had gone into looking good (pseudocommunity) and being right (avoiding chaos) into being real and being whole. This is the safe environment needed for transformation.

Stage Four: Community

The hard work pays off. There is a peace, a sense of contentment, a deep belonging. This is the "container of emergence" that allows a person to feel so safe, knowing that her dark and light sides are seen and accepted, and she can begin to truly blossom. A woman speaks from her heart, personally and responsibly. There is a deep listening born out of emptiness, for the listeners' agendas are cleared and they are completely present for the speaker.

In community, people's differences are neither hidden nor highlighted. They are known and accepted, even at times valued. The group can use the gifts of individuals because now people are comfortable with recognizing they are different. We have seen new parts of people burst forth in the incubator of community. Someone who has struggled with the pain of being stuck in a lifeless marriage for ten years suddenly reports she is seeing a counselor. Another who has been dying to quit her job for five years and start her own business announces to the group that she has handed in her resignation letter. Someone else who has been yearning to work in theater again but has felt overwhelmed by family responsibilities tells us that she is choreographing a play. Two people who never before saw themselves as authors vow to write a book together to share the experience of women's circles. Community is the garden where miracles grow. You get to it by coming through the first

I change myself, I change the world.

....

GLORIA ANZALDÚA

Borderlands / La Frontera

three stages that prepare and fertilize the soil and plant the miracle seeds.

Before leaving these stages, let's clear up one common misunderstanding. You don't pull up in your RV at a town called community as if it were a place to retire. Women's circles are living entities, and they change. You would only be setting yourself up for disappointment if you believed that you could hang out "there" and rest on your laurels. There is no "there" there. As in any relationship—for instance, marriage—you will enjoy periods of peace and joy and happiness, real reveling in yourself and your partner. And then you will experience the other times, of conflict, of struggle, and of emptying. Over time, if groups apply themselves to their focus of spiritual development, they will become better able to go through the hard times comfortably, learning from past experiences and decreasing the amount of denial of and resistance to the inevitable challenges of being together. As Peck notes,

> Community maintenance requires that multiple decisions be made or remade over extensive periods of time. [Who are we? What is our focus? How long is our commitment?] The community will frequently fall back into chaos or even pseudocommunity in the process. Over and again it will need to do the agonizing work of reemptying itself. Many groups fail here. . . . They have forgotten that maintaining themselves as a true community should take priority over all other tasks.

Do you see any parallels with your own individual growth process? We are called to recreate ourselves again and again in our lives. There is no destination at which to arrive. We must ask ourselves the same questions: Who am I? Why am I here? What is important to me? At many stages of our lifetimes, we will feel the chaos. There is no clarity, only struggle. And then comes the emptying of self. What part of me must die for my true self to be reborn? This is the ongoing reincarnation of our souls, the cycle of death and rebirth, that is continually happening inside us.

I believe ordinary Council itself becomes an inner process. In a way each person there is alone, looking into the reflections of herself in the stories, reactions, personalities, and spirits of the other people in the circle. It's like sitting in a circle of mirrors and seeing yourself reflected either directly by people giving you personal feedback, or indirectly by associating with the stories and experiences other people are sharing. . . . So, ordinary Council triggers the inner work because it's an outer manifestation of the collectiveness of Self.

JACK ZIMMERMAN

Dream Network Journal

It Is 7:30 P.M.:
Do You Know Where Your Group Is?

STAGES OF GROUP DEVELOPMENT   QUESTIONS

Pseudocommunity

Is the group in its early stages?

Are relationships cordial but superficial?

Do people generally avoid self-disclosure?

Do people respond to controversial statements with silence?

Do people voice strong opinions and/or feelings?

Is there any open conflict?

Chaos

Does the group seem to focus on people's differences?

Is there a lot of tension and struggle?

Do some people appear to be trying to convince others of their positions?

Emptiness

Are people actively engaged in the process of examining and relinquishing their own blocks to communication and intimacy, for example, expectations, prejudice, fears, need for control?

Is there a sense of parts of the group dying?

Community

Are differences viewed as assets rather than liabilities?

Is there a sense of inclusion?

Do people feel known and safe?

Underlying Problems: The Three Biggies

In our experience three types of underlying problems occur most frequently in women's circles and in groups like them. They are unclear or unagreed-upon group focus, people not taking responsibility for getting their needs met, and unbalanced power dynamics. Each of these symptoms masquerades in many guises, and you may have more than one of them operating at a time. They may raise their ugly heads in any phase of group development. Learning to recognize and address them can save you much time and energy.

Focus

At some point early on you all agreed on the focus of the group or the group intention. Back at the first meeting, the conveners declared their intention, and everyone else assented. But human beings are, by nature, changeable. What once sounded like a great idea can become boring or stale or, at the other extreme, too risky and provocative. Though people may have agreed on a focus, the implications of following through may not have been clear to them until farther down the road. And sometimes people simply forget what they agreed to do.

One group that Sally was in experienced a split between those who wanted an activist orientation and those who wanted to focus on reflection and sharing. In these situations, it is easy to feel frustrated, especially if differences are not openly discussed. It's like trying to drive a car with everyone steering in different directions. We recommend that the group revisit its focus at least once a year to make sure everyone is driving with the same road map.

At the other extreme, the group may lack any single focus, swinging from activism to meditation to study to experience and back. This may not be a problem for some individuals, but others are likely to feel uncomfortable and unclear. Agreeing to and sticking with a focus, even a broad one and even for an agreed-upon period of time, is key in facilitating the formation and the continuance of a group.

Initiation . . . leads from one state of consciousness to another. As each state is entered the horizon enlarges, the vista extends, and the comprehension includes more and more, until the expansion reaches a point where the self embraces all selves.

....
ALICE A. BAILEY

Initiation: Human and Solar

When an individual's needs aren't being met, it is normal for her to feel less motivated to attend the group. Most of us were raised to take what we could get; asking for what we wanted was considered rude. So if we aren't getting what we need, we leave. Again, women's spirituality groups present an opportunity for much *unlearning*. In a twelve-step program, where there is no accountability except perhaps to a higher power, drifting to another meeting may be fine. But in a women's spirituality group, where one of the fundamental principles is taking responsibility for one's own needs, not attending the group without explaining why sabotages yourself and the group.

In fact, chances are that if one group member fails to show regularly, it signals a problem shared by the group that has not yet come to the surface. Encouraging people to ask for what they need from the group not only helps maintain the health of the group, it is good practice for other relationships as well.

When you want from the group something that you aren't getting, whether it is more quiet time or more time in small groups, more ritual, or less ritual, don't hesitate to voice your request. Set aside time in a meeting to find out if others are disenchanted with the group, or some aspect of it, as well. Has the group strayed from its original stated intent? Do you want themes that are less challenging, or more? Ask for what you want. The group may not grant all requests, but it certainly won't have a chance to consider them if they are not ever voiced.

For someone who has taken this journey to the realm of death itself, there is a coming back to the world with gift-bestowing hands. There is a real understanding of oneself, not as a small separate struggling person, but as a part of this whole mystery. There is a breakdown of separateness, a wholeness.

JACK KORNFIELD
Lomi School Bulletin

Power Dynamics

One of the hallmarks of women's spirituality groups is their egalitarianism. Sharing the power and the leadership in the group is a basic practice. There are no more or less important people. Many problems emerge when power becomes unbalanced and one or two people try to run the show.

This doesn't always take the form of the classic power monger seeking control over everyone and everything. In fact, it can start off rather innocently. For example, let's say that Joan and Barbara convened the group. It meets in Barbara's home. Some people started off with the perception that it is Barbara's group. And let's say, further, that Barbara isn't aware of this budding problem. In her excitement and enthusiasm, she is the most vocal proponent of new topics and just generally volunteers a lot. Pretty soon, disgruntled group members start to feel excluded or on the fringe of the group. They may not even understand why they feel marginalized. And suddenly Barbara is starting to seem awfully bossy. Rather than confront her directly with their uncomfortable feelings, they just don't feel like coming anymore, and they start to skip the group. And then there are those phone calls in which group members start gossiping or carping about Barbara.

In this way, insidious little viruses start to weaken groups. The best medicine is to air the problem. Discuss it. Give it oxygen. At the literal level, this is how our bodies combat viruses. The higher the oxygen-carrying capacity of the blood, the more resilient we are in fighting off infections.

Even with a purposeful attempt to equalize power, personalities differ, and it takes consciousness to create and maintain a balance. For instance, both of us have to be careful not to overfunction in our group. Given that the two of us were the conveners of the group, that our work schedules allow us to invest more time into group activities, and that we now have made women's circles our life's work, it would be easy for us to volunteer for everything. However, we try not to put in a lot more energy than others. Jumping in to make things happen may get the immediate task done, but in the long run everyone is shortchanged because the group becomes Sally's and Robin's. We opt for a tad less efficiency and a lot broader ownership of the group.

Conflict Avoidance: All the Seething Little Ladies

Clearly, living in community has its challenges, and being appropriate and straightforward in handling conflict is one of the biggest challenges of all. It's not easy, and few of us have had constructive role models. A common pitfall of women's spirituality groups is to shy away from conflict and to stay in that safe-looking pseudocommunity—the land of white picket fences, Ozzie and Harriet, and *Father Knows Best*. Scott Peck calls this territory inauthentic, boring, sterile, and unproductive. We agree, it's a waste of time.

As women, we may view conflict as one of our worst nightmares. We can smell it a mile away. All our systems to deflect it go on hyperalert. We'd like to escape right back into the sitcoms of the fifties where Donna Reed taught us how to be amiable and not to make trouble. No matter how much work we've done on ourselves to combat our codependence, most of us are loath to do or say something that may hurt someone else. And God forbid that someone should get angry at us or, even worse for many of us, that we should have to experience our anger at another.

So, what do we do? Let's say someone in the group cuts you off repeatedly. Or she is always late and causes a disruption when she arrives. Or she talks incessantly and leads the group off focus. What to do? There's always the "tell a third party what a jerk the person is" ploy. It's called triangulation, and we have all had plenty of practice using it. The person you told passes it on, and soon ugly stuff is happening. People start taking sides, and tension grows between the factions like mold in a damp basement. Who needs it?

In Peck's view, building community really starts when we are willing to deal with pain. If people have the explicit or implicit belief that this group exists to make them happy or safe from all pain, they will be resentful and frustrated when conflict arises. They will, maybe unconsciously, try to push away the conflict because that is not what they think they signed up for. However, the ultimate purpose of any women's circle is *spiritual growth,* and as much as we sometimes would like it to be otherwise, growth spurts rarely happen without pain.

Dealing with conflict in a women's group is great practice for life. It takes guts to bring up a problem with another woman, especially when anger is involved. It takes courage to state your feelings without blaming yourself or anyone else. It is a stretching experience. Becoming more vulnerable is an enormous opportunity for achieving greater intimacy.

Last year Robin had a conflict with Jeanne. Robin was leading a meeting, and Jeanne made a comment that Robin perceived as a thinly veiled criticism. Robin felt angry and resentful. Her first instinct was to go down the triangulation path. And, in fact, she trotted right down it, telling her

I think the reward for conformity is that everyone likes you except yourself.

RITA MAE BROWN

Bingo

mother and sister about her feelings on the way home from the meeting. The judgments and evaluations were flying as she voiced her complaints about Jeanne in the car.

Unfortunately, triangulating didn't alleviate her anger. In fact, it never does. After a few days she still felt hurt and angry. So she decided to take a risk and tell Jeanne how she felt, even though she was scared to do so. Anticipating the confrontation, Robin thought of all the usual reasons for suppressing her feelings and protecting herself. What if Jeanne got angry? What if it ruined her relationship with Jeanne? If she and Jeanne didn't get along, what would it do to the group? And on it went, a litany of convincing, fear-based bull. Simply put, Robin was afraid to tell Jeanne that she was angry about what Jeanne had said.

But Robin did finally call Jeanne and tell her, using "I" statements— what she had heard Jeanne say and how she felt about it. She was careful not to attribute feelings or motivations to Jeanne but only to state her own feelings. Jeanne responded beautifully, acknowledging Robin's feelings and telling her what had prompted her comment in the meeting. It turned out to be something very different from Robin's interpretation. As a result, they became closer than ever rather than carrying the tension of that misunderstanding into the future. Any misunderstanding or conflict that arises in a group requires facing the pain and uncertainty of admitting to unpleasant feelings in order to develop real relationship and real love.

> *Conflict begins at the moment of birth.*
> . . . .
> JEAN BAKER MILLER
> *Toward a New Psychology of Women*

Guidelines for Dealing with Conflict

Talk about the conflict in the most appropriate setting. Conflict can be addressed in the group or outside of it. If the issue is one that seems to involve most people in the group, then it's best to raise it in a meeting. If the conflict is between just two or three people, it probably makes sense to talk about it outside.

Raise the issue as soon as possible. Letting time pass after an incident that causes conflict only allows for resentment and misunderstanding to grow. Also after some time people tend to forget what was actually said or the context in which it was said. Take care of a conflict right away. It usually won't get better all by itself.

Use "I" statements. When you are ready to talk, voice your concerns with "I" statements. "I feel hurt." "I feel angry." Saying "I" makes it clear that you take responsibility for your feelings. You are not attacking or judging, you are expressing your reactions to whatever happened. You don't want to raise the other person's defenses any higher than they already are.

Say how you feel. No one can argue with or invalidate your feelings. Contrary to what we learned as children, feelings are never right or wrong, they just are. Stating feelings is a deceptively simple method of getting the cards on the table. Unfortunately, many of us are unable to perceive what we are actually feeling in the midst of the feelings. Instead, the feelings are suppressed under a whole lot of "shoulds" and "ought tos."

Ask yourself, "Whom does this person represent for me?" If you are really mad at someone, if you are seething, if you are just sure that person is wrong and you are right, you are triggered. That is, "restimulated." How often do we say to ourselves, "I know it is not that big of a deal, but I just can't let go of it"? The person you are angry with probably did something that is triggering an old, emotionally painful pattern in you, and you are not even conscious of it.

For example, Robin has a friend named Sharon. Although most of their relationship is supportive, creative, and fun, one aspect of it really troubled Robin. Sharon would often complain to Robin about how mad she was at someone else. During those conversations, Robin became very uncomfortable and just wanted to get away. Over time, she starting feeling resentful toward Sharon but never said so. In fact, Robin realized it really triggered her and that her reaction was out of proportion to what Sharon was actually doing. When she asked herself, "Whom does Sharon represent for me?," she knew instantly that Sharon reminded her of her mother. When Robin was growing up, her mother complained endlessly about her father and how mean he was. Robin was subjected to countless angry and bitter monologues. She hated it then, and, she now realized, she still hated it. Once she was able to see what was upsetting her so much, the emotional charge of Sharon's anger was diffused for Robin. She still didn't really want to hear Sharon's complaints, but they didn't upset her anymore.

Finally, Robin told Sharon that she didn't like it when Sharon fumed about other people. At first Sharon was hurt. However, after she had time to digest the feedback, Sharon saw that she had not been taking full responsibility for herself when she blamed other people for her problems. Though it was a difficult encounter, the two women both learned about themselves, and their friendship deepened as a result of the conflict.

In this example, Robin asked herself the question "Whom does Sharon represent for me?" Once an adequate level of trust is built in your group, asking this simple but challenging question of one another can be a real gift. When someone is fired up and emotional, she is often experiencing some restimulation from the past. Helping one another identify and clear these issues is extremely healing, and it can be done with trust and sensitivity.

Don't blame yourself or the other person. Remember, no matter how angry or hurt you feel, these are your feelings. No one else is responsible for them but you. Likewise, blaming yourself for how you feel is pointless. All of us have feelings we aren't proud of. Ignoring them does not make them go away.

Address the conflict directly with the person involved— and only with that person. It is so much easier to express anger indirectly, but it can be terribly destructive. Most of us experienced triangulation in our families. Mom would tell us how something that Dad said hurt her, but she didn't tell him, and to top it off she asked us not to tell him, either. Dad would gripe about his issues with Mom but not tell her. Triangulation and secret keeping make up familiar territory for us. However, they solve nothing. At worst, the fault lines of family dysfunction are ever more deeply etched. At best, the problem remains unresolved and resentment builds.

Annual Group Self-Assessment

As in any other communal venture, such as work teams and marriages, consciously taking time to gain perspective and make course corrections is vital. Set aside time once a year to ask questions such as, How are we doing? Where are we going? Such a self-assessment helps to sustain a long-term group. It allows each person to step back and candidly appraise how well the group is serving her needs and purposes, what she is learning, and where she wants the group to go in the future.

As a part of taking care of one's own needs, we highly recommend that anyone speak up at any time if something about the group is bothering her. Such ongoing, spontaneous feedback can be offered as a regular part of meetings. An annual, scheduled assessment is not meant to replace this more informal feedback. Rather, it provides a chance for everyone to speak about her group experience and for the group to decide together where to go next.

Taking the time to focus on how the group is operating can help to uncover and resolve problems that are brewing before they become critical. The assessment helps the group avoid mistaking symptoms for an underlying problem.

Our group learned a lot from our last self-assessment. We set aside a whole evening for this process. One of the most valuable aspects of this session was hearing people share about the group's effects on their lives. The impacts were far greater than we had ever realized. Laura and Robin both said that the group's support had been extremely instrumental in making major job changes. Laura had moved to what at first looked like a wonderful new job as a graphics designer. When it became clear to her that the new workplace was abusive, she was terrified of making yet another change. With the support of the group, she was able to gracefully extricate herself from the new job. Robin quit her high-paying corporate consultant job to develop a dance and yoga program and to write this book.

Bettie said that the group had opened her vistas tremendously through giving her the opportunity to know and love women very different from herself. A traditional homemaker, she became less rigid about some of her ideas on child rearing through witnessing Allison successfully juggle a high-powered job and three small children. It was fascinating and inspiring to hear people describe the long, loving reach the group extends into their lives.

We also discovered that we shared a desire to go deeper with one another. After three solid years of meeting, we felt ready to tackle subjects that were even more challenging. More important, we wanted to create an environment of greater trust so that each person could take more risks in making herself known. This shared desire had not been evident prior to the meeting. Revealing it allowed us to declare our intention to move more deeply into ourselves and into intimacy with one another. One group member has finally disclosed that her husband is HIV-positive, and another has started sharing more about her alcoholic father. We have watched this greater trust and more candid sharing unfold over the past year.

We cannot emphasize the value of taking time to assess your group regularly. It can mean the difference between keeping the group vitally alive or having it end—either with an angry blowup or a slow quiet wheeze. Do a self-assessment before there is a crisis, before the tension has built up, before people have given up, and you'll likely experience a much clearer energy in the group.

HOME
REMEDIES TO
KEEP YOUR
GROUP
HEALTHY
. . . .

Annual Group Self-Assessment Questionnaire

Here is a list of assessment questions we have used. They are by no means exhaustive of the kinds of questions you might want to ask; rather, they are a place to begin. Start by choosing four or five of these questions:

1. What has been the best thing, for you, about being in the group? Why?

2. What aspects of the way the group operates (activities, specific incidents, logistics, dynamics) do not work well for you? Why?

3. Would you have set up the group differently from the start? If so, how?

4. What has been most challenging for you about being in the group? Why?

5. What has been the most painful thing about being in the group? Why?

6. What has been the most nurturing and supportive thing about being in the group?

7. What positive or negative reactions have you had to group dynamics?

8. Do you perceive factions, or subgroups, within the group, and how does that feel to you?

9. Is the group especially dependent upon a certain person or persons for ideas, leadership, resources, permission?

10. How has being in the group affected your life?

11. What conflicts do you see existing in the group?

12. How do you see these conflicts being addressed, if at all?

13. What about the power issues in the group? Are you comfortable with the way that power is distributed?

14. What is your sense of the trust level in the group? Is it deep or not? Why?

15. Do you have needs or interests that are not being met by your participation in the group that you would like to have met? What are they?

16. Where would you like to see the group go in the next six months? The next year? Should we adjust or change the focus?

17. To what extent has the group been accepting of differences and able to draw on the special gifts of each member?

18. If not already stated, is there any way you would like the group to change in the next year?

How to Use the Questionnaire

You can go about the assessment in many different ways. We like to mail the questions out ahead of time so that people will be able to think about them before they come to the meeting. You might ask people to write down the answers, but this doesn't work well for our low-maintenance group because people rebel against this much homework. Depending on the size of the group, you could split into smaller groups so that each person has more time to speak to each question. After the small groups are finished discussing the questions, reconvene with everyone and share the major themes or learnings from the discussion. Leave plenty of time, at least two and one-half hours, so that you can explore the questions deeply rather than treat them in a cursory manner.

We recommend taking notes or taping this session. Have a volunteer capture the highlights, write them up, and circulate them. It will help to reinforce the group learning. In retrospect, we wish we had taped our meetings consistently. Invariably someone is absent and would love to hear a tape of the session.

When Women Leave the Group

Out of fifteen original group members, four have left the group. Elizabeth was the first to leave. Her work responsibilities and the stress of running a large fund-raising campaign for the nonprofit she heads left her too busy to continue with us. Liz #2 lost her job as a managed health care executive and moved to Long Island to live with her new love. Lois, after several years of severe depression, finally sold her house, pulled herself together, and followed her bliss out West, where she found an adobe house outside of Taos. And Robin's sister Clair moved to the Philadelphia area to live in a safe and beautiful community away from the city. Each of these transitions left a hole in the group.

We didn't handle the first two departures very well. We just let them go without much fanfare. We never acknowledged our sadness or the feeling that we would miss them. When a group bonds as tightly as ours has, with members investing so much of themselves in group meetings, it is no small matter when a member leaves. It's a loss, and acting like it's no big deal will not be satisfying in the long run. Of course, most of us have been conditioned to believe that such a loss is no big deal and, even when it is a big deal, that it is not socially acceptable to make a fuss about it. Whether or not we want to face it, group members leaving brings up, consciously or unconsciously, loss and abandonment issues from our pasts. This, of course, in addition to the current pain of losing the companionship of someone we love and care for. So when people leave a group, it is worth paying attention. Departures are a chance for conscious closure.

Naturally, we recommend creating a ritual for the leave-taking. It needn't be an elaborate one. Our group enjoys very simple rituals. See chapter 7, "Reclaiming Ritual," for a full treatment of how we use ritual. In the instance of a member leaving, the ritual can help to bring closure and to provide a vehicle for people to express their love and appreciation for the departing member.

Clair and Lois left at the same time and attended the same final meeting. The two of us were the "mothers" for the meeting. It was our responsibility to plan the evening, and the overall theme was the harvest. It was, naturally, our August meeting. We had asked everyone ahead of time to bring a symbolic gift for Clair and Lois and to be ready to say a few words to speed them on their journey. The simple ritual that evolved spontaneously was exquisite and heartfelt. After going around the circle and sharing the gifts, we played a tape of the song "You Have a Place in My Heart," by The Sounds of Blackness. Within short order, the group had dissolved into warm tears and hugs. It was one of the most moving meetings we have ever had.

Celebrations and Lots of Them

Our last home remedy for groups (and for life in general) is to celebrate together and to do it often. It is so easy, especially in workaholic Washington, D.C., to make everything hard work. We keep tackling the hard jobs, keep working on problems, and keep the attention on what hasn't happened yet.

Instead, celebrate things. Celebrate that it is June. Celebrate a person's new job. Celebrate a new baby, a new home, a birthday, your breasts, any passage, large or small. Celebrating is an acknowledging of what is good and right and wonderful. It puts our attention on what we have accomplished, what windfalls have happened, and what is just right.

When we submitted the last draft of this book, we celebrated by taking a walk under the cherry trees near the Jefferson Memorial here in

Washington. We made a little paper boat and released it into the waters of the Tidal Basin, thus symbolizing our intention for the book to reach many people and the letting go of our attachment to how that may happen. It was a small private celebration and very satisfying.

HOME
REMEDIES TO
KEEP YOUR
GROUP
HEALTHY
. . . .

How, you might wonder, can we celebrate all these things and still get to the heart of the meeting? Well, try "quickie" celebrations. Do it fast and with flair. It took only five minutes for us to do our topless "breast appreciation" ritual to celebrate the end of Sandra's radiation treatments and the health of our breasts. But it is something none of us will never forget! One group we know actually ends each meeting by having each person recount all the miracles, big and small, that have occurred in her life since the last meeting. We want to adopt this ourselves.

Of course, we don't advise groups to avoid dealing with pain, illness, suffering, and stuckness. But don't forget the lighter side. Celebrating together fosters a grateful heart and helps us remember why we're together. We are renewed and restored by joy and acknowledgment.

. . . .

Keeping a group going is a labor of love. As with a relationship, it requires patience, devotion, and a willingness to be vulnerable, to confront problems head-on. Just because we are women, and just because it's a spirituality group, doesn't guarantee that it will always be sweetness and light. To the contrary, that is precisely the model of spirituality that we are trying to get away from.

The moral of this story is: **Being willing to bring up and talk about the seemingly small stuff will keep your group healthier in the long run than anything else you can do!** "Real" women *do* get angry and express their feelings. Our group has been remarkably free from conflict among ourselves. Sometimes we wonder if this is due to our "nice girl" conditioning. We probably have more than a little of it. We are all still learning to trust our feelings and our intuition and to express ourselves responsibly. Robin has asked to lead our next meeting focusing on the stages of community development and how and where we see ourselves in these stages. This should stir the pot!

Being in spiritual community is saying yes to life in a big way. Saying yes and jumping naked into the ocean of relationship. Some of those waves are big and intimidating, but as we learn to ride them, they can be thrilling. One of our favorite sources of inspiration, Hildegard of Bingen, defined sin as being "dried up." We'd rather have juicy lives, even if they get messy at times. Come on in. The water is . . . wet.

A Sacred Scenario

> *Women are remembering the cellular structure of original*
> *community and are seeking ways to circle back to reconnection.*
> *The missing core in all our self-searching may be community:*
> *our ability to trust each other enough to inter/act and stay*
> *bonded as we learn how to reweave the web of the world.*
>
> MUSAWA,
> *We'moon Calendar '97*

Some quick vignettes:

A seven-year-old is fondled by her uncle and is threatened if she tells anyone.

A twelve-year-old starts her first period and anxiously obsesses about making sure that her family and friends don't find out. She is deeply humiliated when her father asks her about it.

A young teenager irons her hair to straighten it.

A high school student dumbs herself down by pretending not to know the answers in class so as not to appear too smart.

A fourteen-year-old reluctantly agrees to have sex with her boyfriend, thinking it's the only way to keep him interested in her and away from her friends.

A sixteen-year-old endures the pain of childbirth alone in the hospital.

A teenager is instructed on the techniques of a new diet aid—vomiting after a binge. The person teaching her how to purge is her mother.

A Peace Corps volunteer is raped at gunpoint in the African rainforest by a "friend," the husband of her new boss.

A woman and her young son are threatened with a gun by a very intoxicated angry husband.

A forty-year-old woman has a hysterectomy because the obstetrician tells her that she doesn't need her "baby carriage" anymore.

These incidents all happened to the two of us. We are far from unique. These are not, by any stretch of the imagination, unusual. Rather, they are the norm. We didn't know any better. We don't blame ourselves anymore. We didn't understand that our uncles didn't have the right to stick their fingers inside of us, that our uteruses were more than baby carriages. Our mothers and grandmothers didn't know, either. They weren't willfully hiding from us the love and support we needed to journey through and to the unknown. Their mothers simply hadn't taught them much about menstruation but, instead, had unintentionally shamed them about their bodies, buying them their first corsets and girdles. Our mothers and grandmothers taught that women needed to appear weak in order to attract strong men.

Even though we are starting to learn better, many of the myths of womanhood persist to this day. We may be wearing sweatpants instead of girdles, but our minds are still under the sway of the myth of the weaker sex. These myths exert their powerful grip on us as long as we remain unconscious of them. We don't experience them as myths but rather as reality, the way things really are. What are some of the myths that you live by?

Take the myth surrounding menstruation. Women have always bled. Few of us were actually told by our mothers that this was a dirty, smelly time of the month, but the cultural myth was nevertheless shrieking that message to us through its "feminine hygiene" products. Deodorize, cover up, control. What if we had grown up with an alternate myth—a myth that celebrated the monthly flow instead of trying to staunch it? We might even believe that menstruation could be a time of special powers for women, a time to relax and surrender into the shedding of the uterine wall. There are women who have reclaimed their menses as a normal part of their bodies' cyclical changing nature. Believe it or not, there are cultures that have no word in their language for PMS and no concept of menstrual pain.

Myths are constructs—paradigms that have developed over time. Myths both reflect and determine reality. They are the stories that underpin our culture, the invisible structures that we hang our lives on. We can easily become trapped in these myths, and most of us are ensnared at least some of the time. No wonder we feel like we are leading someone else's life or that we have become a marginal character in our own story, a walk-on in our spouses' and children's lives. In order to reclaim center stage, we need to start inventing new myths as well as reclaiming the ancient ones. What if we started living out of new myths?

One set of new myths is being created out of discoveries about the egalitarian, Goddess-worshiping cultures of prehistory. But even the archaeological artifacts, so valiantly uncovered and interpreted by the Marija Gimbutases and Riane Eislers of this century, do not, in and of themselves, reveal the whole picture. They are necessary but not sufficient. It is critical for us to learn that there was a time when the divine was seen as feminine and when neither men nor women dominated. But this perspective does not provide a full template for a new society even though it does challenge the prevailing paradigms of male supremacy and patriarchal deities. It seems that there was a time, not so long ago, when things were very different. Therefore they can be different again. It is this spark of creative dissonance that kindles our imaginations, moving us to develop new myths and new realities.

And once the imagination has been kindled, we begin to see choices that we had never even seen before . . . like giving birth at home surrounded by loving friends or exchanging tampons for cotton menstrual pads or creating our own rituals to celebrate life's passages or not allowing our sons and daughters to be circumcised. But just seeing that we have different options and choices rarely gives us the strength we need to exercise these options. For this we need more than imagination. We need the courage to reach beyond ourselves, extending our hands to one another and to powers that are greater than ourselves. Women's spirituality groups have become the matrix for this creative and conscious unfolding. For a future to be possible, a future that we can be proud of leaving to our children and their children, women need to claim spiritual authority and to accept spiritual responsibility for this planet. We must become teachers for each other.

In talking to hundreds of women as we wrote this book, we noted that one conversation in particular gave us a gigantic dose of "what if." Sally was telling her friend Karen about her group. Karen, in turn, wanted Sally to know about her women's circle in Nashville. They meet for dinner at a local restaurant on the fourth Tuesday of every month. Serendipitously, and after months of struggling to align on a date each month, our group had also landed on the fourth Tuesday of each month as a regular meeting date. "'Wow," Karen exclaimed, "what if every- where on the planet women all met together on the fourth Tuesday of every month?" This possibility has captured our imagination. We invite each of you to suggest to your group that you try meeting on the fourth Tuesday of each month. There's no telling what could happen!

Imagine this . . . It is the fourth Tuesday of the month. You are sitting with your small circle of women friends. Your group is but one of mil- lions meeting all over the planet. You have been given the power to look down on our world from above, enjoying the perspective that our astro- nauts have had. You can see the land masses, the great rivers, the moun- tains and the tropical forests, and the water surrounding everything. Just imagine for a few seconds what this looks like. The earth, hanging against the inky dark backdrop of space. You watch the continents, green and brown, drift past. You see the thinnest of membranes separating the earth's atmosphere from outer space. . . .

Suddenly you begin to notice tiny little flickering lights all over the land surface of the earth, blue and white flickering lights. As you look longer, you begin to notice tiny delicate filaments connecting these lights to one another, a jeweled network, like a spiderweb drenched in the early morning dew. This network gently pulsates and throbs as en- ergy flows through it, each tiny light its own energy source. The web slowly begins to come into focus against the backdrop of the earth, like one of those holographic hidden pictures that suddenly leaps into view. You can be looking at the picture and never even imagine it there, but by relaxing your gaze, the hidden esoteric overlay reveals itself.

You move closer to the earth, very close in fact, in order to fathom this mysterious web. Just what is generating this pulsating light? When you get close enough to see the source, you can no longer see the pattern that connects all the lights. No matter, you will be able to recapture the broader perspective later. The light seems to be coming from a hut or a home or a clearing. You move in closer to get a better look. You see a simple circle of women, sitting together around a lovely center point that is decorated with fruit and candles. You hear their laughter, raucous at times, then the quiet intensity of focused listening as each woman speaks in turn. The energy generated by the listening is palpable! You realize this intense listening is the source of the light, which flickers and pulsates depending on the depth and quality of the listening. You are suddenly able to see the energy swirling around the circle, healing and restoring each woman as she speaks and is listened into wholeness.

Now you begin to move out, away from this one particular group. Suddenly another group appears on the next block, then another and another, each with its own swirl of energy. This energy, as it becomes more intense, starts to jump out of its confines, seeking to hook up with the larger energetic pattern, the invisible power grid connecting all these groups to one another. The charge becomes stronger as it leaps from town to town, effortlessly jumping geographical and political boundaries, gaining in vibrational intensity and resonating at a higher and higher frequency as women all over the planet share their stories and tell their truths.

The network of feminine wisdom. This is our network. This is our natural home, where we really belong. It is here that we can always tap into this wisdom, energy, and love. As long as we listen to each other.

Afterword
No One but Us

> There is no one but us. There is no one to send, nor a clean
> hand, nor a pure heart on the face of the earth, nor in the
> earth, but only us, a generation comforting ourselves with the
> notion that we have come at an awkward time, that our
> innocent fathers are all dead—as if innocence had ever
> been—and our children busy and troubled, and we ourselves
> unfit, not yet ready, having each of us chosen wrongly,
> made a false start, failed, yielded to impulse and the
> tangled comfort of pleasures, and grown exhausted,
> unable to seek the thread, weak and involved. But
> there is no one but us. There never has been.
>
> ANNIE DILLARD,
> *Holy the Firm*

A fairly typical phenomenon takes place when new social movements arise. When a new movement challenges the dominant culture, as the movement of developing women's sacred circles surely does, people get uncomfortable. They try to label and fit the new development into a familiar category. "Oh, I know," they'll say, "it's like those CR groups my mother was in during the seventies." Women worship the moon, they must be witches. They meet with women only, they must hate men. Stereotypes are thereby born.

In the case of women's spirituality, we are talking about something that fundamentally threatens the established values of the dominant culture. When a phenomenon like sacred circles comes along, you can be sure that not only will its ideas and contributions be oversimplified, but that it will actually be misrepresented so as to appear as repugnant, dangerous, and un-American as possible.

Just look at how skillfully Rush Limbaugh delegitimized feminism with the term *femiNazi*. Linking fascism with a diverse group of women who believe in equality—now that was a clever way to make sure all kinds of women keep feminism at arm's length, even women who wouldn't dream of listening to Rush.

We laugh, but what actually happens when such stereotyping occurs? We think what happens is that women who share similar concerns, dreams, and values lose their connection to one another and to the power that comes from that connection. Women who deeply desire a bright future of unfettered opportunity for their daughters are struck with fear at being associated with "those women." "Those women," who are selfish, mean-spirited, rigid, angry, and alienated man haters. "Those women" become the enemy, and we shrink back into our singularity. We allow ourselves to be fragmented by fear when we accept stereotypes as the way things are. This does nothing but slow the process of individual and social change. Rather than focusing on the common bonds of womanhood, we focus on keeping a safe distance from "those women."

As women's spirituality becomes a more prominent force of individual and social change in the years ahead, we can expect the assaults on it to become more pronounced. Witness the lacerating criticism of Hillary Rodham Clinton for consulting with Jean Houston and Mary Catherine Bateson. As we become more powerful, the need to suppress us will become stronger.

We ask you to be aware of this dynamic and to resist the inclination to renounce your sisters when you sense the divide-and-conquer tactic being employed. When times seem unsure, always reconnect to your sense of inner knowing. You will then be guided by love rather than fear. And remember, *there is no one but us.*

Circle Resources

BOOKS

Both of us are serious and avid readers. We read not only for learning and entertainment, but also as a form of spiritual practice. For us, reading has been a primary vehicle for spiritual development. Reading a Rumi poem or an essay by Terry Tempest Williams is a surefire way to connect with the divine. This book list represents a fraction of what is available in the arena of women's spirituality. It is neither exhaustive nor complete; it is rather a sampling of our favorites and the ones we have found the most helpful as we have written this book and worked with women's circles.

We recommend that you go to a bookstore that has a good women's or new age section. Is there a book that falls off the shelf as you approach or one that grabs your attention? That's an unscientific but usually satisfying place to start. We call it "intuitive research," and it's been our primary research tool.

Women's Spirituality

The Feminine Face of God, by Sherry Ruth Anderson and Patricia Hopkins. New York: Bantam Books, 1991. Our favorite book on all the different manifestations of women's spirituality, with richly detailed stories from some wonderful role models.

A Circle of Stones, by Judith Duerk. San Diego: LuraMedia, 1989. An evocative, self-guided journey to the archetypal feminine written from a Jungian perspective.

Living in the Lap of the Goddess: The Feminist Spirituality Movement in America, by Cynthia Eller. Boston: Beacon Press, 1994. Through interviews, participant observation, and analysis of movement literature, Eller explores what women who worship the Goddess believe.

The Women's Retreat Book, by Jennifer Louden. San Francisco: HarperSanFrancisco, 1997. All the tools for taking yourself away from the hurly-burly of daily life. Well organized, thoughtful, and full of inspiring stories.

A God Who Looks Like Me: Discovering A Woman-Affirming Spirituality, by Patricia Lynn Reilly. New York: Ballantine Books, 1995. A guide to reframing Christian theology in a way that honors women. Especially helpful for those emerging from harsh religious traditions.

Keys to the Open Gate, by Kimberly Snow. Berkeley: Conari Press, 1994. A rich collection of readings on topics as varied as goddesses, Taoist and Buddhist meditation, rape, and creativity. Lots of wonderful quotes.

Revolution from Within, by Gloria Steinem. Boston: Little, Brown, 1992. The first mainstream book to link the political to the psychological to the spiritual and to argue emphatically for the necessity of spiritual development as a basis for political and social change.

Four Centuries of Jewish Women's Spirituality: A Sourcebook, edited by Ellen M. Umansky and Dianne Ashton. Boston: Beacon Press, 1992. A fascinating compendium of Jewish women, from ancient times to the present, speaking about spirituality. Very inspiring for women of any religious background.

Creating Community and Group Process

Calling the Circle: The First and Future Culture, by Christina Baldwin. Newberg, OR: Swan Raven, 1994. Recommended by our friend and mentor, Colleen Kelley, Baldwin's book not only teaches about the council process, it also tells some compelling stories.

The Different Drum: Community Making and Peace, by M. Scott Peck, M.D. New York: Simon & Schuster, 1987. A fantastic book on community that simultaneously deglamorizes and exalts its subject with fascinating observations on the stages of spiritual development in individuals and groups. We have borrowed heavily from Peck's work. Thank you.

The Way of Council, by Jack Zimmerman in collaboration with Virginia Coyle. Las Vegas: Bramble Books, 1996. Council-style sharing is a foundational practice in women's spirituality groups, and this is the definitive handbook on council process as practiced and refined for the last twenty years at the Ojai Foundation. This remarkable center in California has become one of the confluence points of Native American practices and Buddhist wisdom teachings.

Sources for Inspirational Readings

Sisters of the Earth: Women's Prose and Poetry About Nature, edited by Lorraine Anderson. New York: Vintage, 1991. Healing and appealing selection from the best women nature writers of this century. The bibliography alone is worth the price of the book.

Each Day a New Beginning: Daily Meditations for Women, by Anonymous. Center City, MN: Hazelden, 1982. Full of wisdom and compassion. Will inspire you to put your own needs first.

The Essential Rumi, translated by Coleman Barks. San Francisco: HarperSanFrancisco, 1995. Robin's all-time favorite poet and right up there for Sally, too, Rumi captures the mysticism, playfulness, paradox, irony, and the divine in the everyday. There are poems for just about every mood and occasion.

Daughters of Copper Woman, by Anne Cameron. Vancouver, BC: Press Gang, 1981. Now a classic, this tale will initiate you into the ways of wise women. We read excerpts from this at one of our very first meetings.

Gift from the Sea, by Anne Morrow Lindbergh. New York: Vintage, 1955. Wise musings on the connections between the natural and the everyday world. An enduring best-seller and still one of our favorites for inspiration.

Holy the Firm, by Annie Dillard. New York: Harper & Row, 1977. Achingly beautiful writing as Dillard observes moths immolating themselves in candle flame, the sun rising over the eastern Cascades, and other happenings from her little cabin. All of her books are wonderful.

Being Home and *Journeying in Place,* by Gunilla Norris. New York: Bell Tower, 1991 and 1994. Exquisitely written, these modern classics dwell on the sacred in the everyday. They make you want to plant bulbs, wax floors, and hand-dry the dishes.

Earth Prayers, edited by Elizabeth Roberts and Elias Amidon. San Francisco: HarperSanFrancisco, 1991. Three hundred sixty-five prayers, poems, and invocations from around the world. This lovely, well-organized compendium lets you find a prayer for the equinox or a saint's day or a benediction for your animals.

Life Prayers: 365 Prayers, Blessings, and Affirmations to Celebrate the Human Journey, another gift from Elizabeth Roberts and Elias Amidon. San Francisco: HarperSanFrancisco, 1996. Exquisite poems and prose for rites of passage and every other day.

Cries of the Spirit, edited by Marilyn Sewell. Boston: Beacon Press, 1991. A treasure. Wonderful well-edited collection of poems by all of our great women poets.

An Unspoken Hunger, by Terry Tempest Williams. New York: Pantheon, 1994. Williams is one of our finest living nature writers. Her prose is even better read aloud. We read these essays to each other by flashlight on a wilderness retreat, fairly hugging ourselves with delight.

Other Resource Guides

Altars Made Easy: A Complete Guide to Creating Your Own Sacred Space, by Peg Streep. San Francisco: HarperSanFrancisco, 1997.

Goddesses and Wise Women: The Literature of Feminist Spirituality 1980–1992, An Annotated Bibliography, by Anne Carson. Freedom, CA: Crossing Press, 1992. We stumbled across this gem on our first trip to the Library of Congress and ordered it immediately. A comprehensive listing of 1,002 publications(!).

Motherpeace: A Way to the Goddess Through Myth, Art and Tarot, by Vicki Noble. San Francisco: HarperSanFrancisco, 1983. This is not just another how-to book on tarot cards. It's full of history, mythology, and all manner of juicy wisdom.

The Woman Source Catalog and Review: Tools for Connecting the Community of Women, edited by Ilene Rosoff, managing editor of The Launch Pad. Berkeley: Celestial Arts, 1995. A "whole earth" encyclopedic approach to much more than women's spirituality.

The Womanspirit Sourcebook, edited by Patrice Wynn. San Francisco: HarperSan-Francisco, 1988. Out of print and worth hunting down. Lovingly put together by the proprietor, staff, and friends of Gaia, the incredible woman's bookstore in Berkeley, this is the ultimate annotated bibliography. Reviews of and essays about all the classics of women's spirituality and interviews with their writers.

Goddess Culture

The Chalice and the Blade, by Riane Eisler. San Francisco: HarperSanFrancisco, 1987. One of the pivotal works that reframes our entire understanding of culture, especially in formulating the "dominator" and "partnership" models and how they have emerged throughout history and prehistory.

The Language of the Goddess, by Marija Gimbutas. San Francisco: HarperSan-Francisco, 1989. A classic by a pioneering archaeologist who presents prolific evidence of the prepatriarchal cultures in Europe and Asia that worshiped God in female forms.

The Great Cosmic Mother: Rediscovering the Religion of the Earth, by Monica Sjöö and Barbara Mor. San Francisco: HarperSanFrancisco, 1991. Wonderful illustrations by Monica Sjöö. Radical thinking and penetrating scholarship make this a challenging book. Insightful and inciting!

The Women's Encyclopedia of Myths and Secrets, by Barbara Walker. San Francisco: HarperSanFrancisco, 1983. An astonishing compendium, this feminist encyclopedia covers mythology, anthropology, women's wisdom, sexuality, and more, with 1,350 entries. Full of prepatriarchal tidbits.

Earth-Based Spirituality, Witchcraft, and Paganism

Drawing Down the Moon, by Margot Adler. Boston: Beacon Press, 1979. A rich, colorful description of paganism in America, replete with lots of interviews by lively, interesting folks.

The Sacred Hoop: Recovering the Feminine in American Indian Traditions, by Paula Gunn Allen. Boston: Beacon Press, 1986. A collection of essays, by one of our Native elders and University of California professor, reclaiming the contributions, traditions, values, and vision of Native American foremothers.

The Four-Fold Way, by Angeles Arrien, Ph.D. San Francisco: HarperSanFrancisco, 1993. Very accessible book on the basics of earth-based spirituality across many cultures.

Creating Circles of Power and Magic: A Woman's Guide to Sacred Community, by Caitlin Libera. Freedom, CA: Crossing Press, 1994. This book, in the pagan/Wiccan tradition, tells the story of a particular group, describes its processes and rituals, and asks thought-provoking questions to help readers in creating their own circles.

The Spiral Dance: A Rebirth of the Ancient Religion of the Great Goddess, by Starhawk. San Francisco: Harper & Row, 1979. Complete with exercises, meditations, spells, and charms, this classic has given women access to secrets long suppressed.

Life's Companion: Journal Writing as a Spiritual Quest, by Christina Baldwin. New York: Bantam Books, 1991. Journals are a primary tool for women exploring their spirituality. This thoughtful book will inspire journal keepers to new heights of journaling. It picks up where Julia Cameron leaves off with morning pages.

Composing a Life, by Mary Catherine Bateson. New York: Penguin, 1990. Life as an improvisational art form, making it up as we go along, through the biographies of five women, including Bateson, the daughter of Margaret Mead and the confessor of Hillary Rodham Clinton.

The Artist's Way, by Julia Cameron. New York: Putnam, 1992. A life changer! This book can help you to manifest any project, idea, vision, work of art, or part of yourself. It is a profound, funny, accessible, and highly practical workbook on making your dreams come true. Use it!

Bird by Bird: Some Instructions on Writing and Life, by Anne Lamott. New York: Pantheon Books, 1994. Anyone can love and learn from this hilarious, touching book on doing what you love. We can never repay the gratitude we feel for her notion of the "shitty first draft," which is transferable to most situations in life.

Maps to Ecstasy: Teachings of an Urban Shaman, by Gabrielle Roth. San Rafael, CA: New World Library, 1989. This freeing and provocative book was written by a master movement shaman. You don't have to be a dancer, just have a body, to benefit from it.

MUSIC

We love music and use it constantly as a way of altering consciousness. The following list is our spiritual hit parade. We have tried to separate the items in terms of meditative music, which you also can move to if you wish, and more rowdy stuff that you won't be able to sit still for. Enjoy! And make sure you turn it up loud!

Music for Meditation and Listening: Sitting Music

Amazing Grace, Aretha Franklin. Incredible gospel numbers, several of which are pretty nonsectarian and deliriously soulful.

Ancient Mother, On Wings of Song and Robbie Gass. A full women's choir singing ancient and modern love songs to Her.

Anonymous 4, all their records. This quartet sings heavenly a capella medieval music. Very calming.

ABoneCroneDrone, Sheila Chandra. Very mesmerizing, hypnotic. Good for slow movement and guided meditations and visualizations.

The Changer and the Changed, Cris Williamson. The record that initiated many of us into women's music. It still soars.

Dead Can Dance. We like all their records, some for meditation, some for moving.

Enya, all her records. Airy, watery, floaty music by a contemporary Celtic queen.

Echoes of Nature, Frog Chorus. Quiet chirping.

Garden of Ecstasy, Kay Gardner. A pioneer composer and performer of women's music.

Global Meditations, a four-volume anthology of sacred world music.

Skeleton Woman, Flesh and Bone. These wonderful musicians, including Peter Kater, David Darling, and Chris White, weave a spell using a Clarissa Pinkola Estés story. No lyrics, just deep feeling.

Le Mystère des Voix Bulgares. Ethereal, layered music.

Loreena McKennitt, everything she has produced. Celtic, dreamy, powerful, and trance inducing.

Medicine Woman, Medwyn Goodall. Grounding, soothing, instrumental music.

Migration, Peter Kater and R. Carlos Nakai. Much of our book was written with this incredibly beautiful music playing in the background. It will take you away.

Mustt Mustt and Night Song, Nusrat Fateh Ali Khan. Said to have the broadest vocal range of any singer in recent memory, Khan produced a very un-Western sound that is thoroughly affecting.

A Place in the World, Mary Chapin Carpenter. Several great cuts, including "A Sudden Gift of Fate," "A Place in the World," "What If We Went to Italy?" and "Ideas Are Like Stars."

Renewal of Spirit, Debbie Friedman. Beautiful healing folk songs in English and Hebrew.

Sacred Space Music, Constance Demby. Celestial hammered dulcimer.

Sea Peace, Georgia Kelly. Transcendental harp.

Trance Planet (Volumes 1–3), various artists. Excellent international music with a spiritual/mystical spin. Good for slow movement and meditations.

Tuck and Patti, anything they have produced. This husband-wife team (guitar and vocalist, respectively) composes and performs uplifting, soulful music.

Wa Le La, Rita Coolidge, Laura Satterfield, and Priscilla Coolidge. Haunting blend of Native American and women's music.

Paul Winter, anything he has produced, especially when he sings with wolves and whales.

Upbeat and Feisty: Moving Music

Beggars and Saints, Jai Uttal. Uttal has taken Hindu music and seasoned it with a little rock 'n' roll and some bluegrass. Quite intoxicating.

Deep Forest, everything they produce. Mystical, gutsy new age music from the jungle.

Journey of the Drum, Sounds of Blackness. Amazing sound from a huge gospel choir that combines traditional spirituals, drumming, and even some good hip-hop.

Native Wisdom: World Music of the Spirit, various artists. A wonderful international collection with some great drumming cuts.

New Beginnings, Tracy Chapman. "I'm Ready" is one of the most delicious songs of initiation we've ever heard.

Babatunde Olatunji, everything he has produced. Nigerian traditional drumming, great for dancing.

Le Roi Est Mort, Vive Le Roi, Enigma. Engaging blend of medieval choirs, drums, and space music. Groovy!

Planet Drum, Mickey Hart and friends. Great drumming cuts of differing tempos.

Ragas and Sagas, Jan Gabarek and Ustad Fateh Ali Khan. Indian instrumental music with a twist.

Gabrielle Roth, everything she has produced. Great for drumming and free movement.

Shaman's Breath, Professor Trance and the Energizers. Great, wild drumming.

Sweet Honey in the Rock, all their work. This fiercely musical and un-abashedly political African American women's a capella group belts out songs that get you up and moving.

Yeha Noha, Sacred Spirits. Native American music with a new age and rock spin.

When I Was a Boy, Jane Siberry. Hard to describe, this woman is out there! Her song "Calling All Angels," sung with k. d. lang, is tremendous. Mystical, funny, and warm, with a few hard edges; take a listen.

WOMEN'S SPIRITUALITY
IN CYBERSPACE

There is a lot of activity on the Internet concerning women's spirituality. In a brief perusal, we found chat rooms, companies that sell ritual supplies and goddess statues, bibliographies, and all manner of fascinating sites to explore. The rate of change is astronomical, and the likelihood of anything we recommend being there next week, much less a year from now, is slim.

We are relative novices on the Web, but we are lucky enough to know some true experts. These wise folks have shared with us some pointers on how to find material related to women's spirituality.

Here's how to search the World Wide Web using the powerful search tools:

Internet Directory. Yahoo is one of the Internet directories @ http://www.yahoo.com. When you get there you can look under *spirituality* and *women* and see what is available. You can click on the sites directly.

Search Engines. Lycos (http://www.lycos.com) and *Webcrawler* (http://webcrawler.com) are both tools for searching the Internet using key words. Again, *women* and *spirituality* would be a good start. You might try adding other key words, like *Jewish* or *pagan*.

Finally, we know the people at *Voices of Women,* a cyber resource guide and magazine that focuses on women's spirituality. Their Web site (http://www.voiceofwomen.com) is linked to hundreds of women's and women's spirituality sites. Their health and wellness site is called *Whole Living* (http://wholeliving.com). They assure us they will be around for a long time. Happy surfing.

SUPPLIES

We use lots candles, incense, and fragrant essential oils. You should be able to find high quality supplies locally. If not, a business opportunity awaits you! A tremendous amount of resources is available on the World Wide Web, through the Internet. Just go to a "Search" engine, type in a word like *incense,* and you will be amazed at all the references. Many women-owned mail-order businesses are listed. Kind of like a giant, intergalactic yellow pages. Try using them.

Here is a wonderful supplier we use:

Shenandoah Shamanic Resources, Eka Kapiotis Bull and Ed Bull, Front Royal, VA 22630. email: eebull@rma.edu 1–800–455–2087. Call for catalog.

FILM AND VIDEO

We haven't seen all these films, but some of them look too tantalizing to leave out of this guide.

Judy Chicago: The Birth Project, Vivian Kleiman, director; Frances Reid, cinematography. 1985. 20 minutes. Vivian Kleiman Productions, dist., 2600 10th St., Berkeley, CA 94710. 415–549–1470. Explores the theme of human birth as a metaphor for the creation of the universe. One hundred fifty needle-workers from across the country created this collective piece honoring the most central women's experience.

Miriam's Daughters Now: Jewish Women's New Rituals, Lilly Rivlin, producer/director/writer. 1986. 29 minutes. El Ar Film Productions, dist., 463 West St., Suite 510A, New York, NY 10014. Leading Jewish feminists gathered to create women-honoring rituals, thereby shaping a place for themselves within the tradition. Featuring Letty Cottin Pogrebin, Bella Abzug, and Esther Broner.

Quilts in Women's Lives, Pat Ferrero. 1980. 28 minutes. New Day Films, dist., 22 Riverview Drive, Wayne, NJ 07470. 212–477–4604. The film profiles seven diverse women quiltmakers, examining their spiritual values and inspiration for their art.

Goddess Remembered, The Burning Times, and *Full Moon,* Donna Read. National Film Board of Canada. 1–800–542–2164 to order. The Canadian filmmaker Donna Read has made a brilliant and inspiring trilogy of hour-long films. *Full Circle* draws on the customs, rites, and knowledge of the past to envision a sustainable future where domination is replaced with respect. At the center of all these films is a reverence for the earth. *The Burning Times* is an in-depth look at the witch hunts that swept Europe just a few hundred years ago. The film advances the theory that widespread violence against women and the neglect of our environment today can be traced back to those times.

OUR FAVORITE PLACES TO RETREAT
AND TO MEET KINDRED SPIRITS

We just couldn't complete this guide without sharing some of our favorite places for spiritual retreat and renewal. Whether you go with your group, with a friend, or alone, these are truly magical places to take yourself.

Kripalu Center for Yoga and Health, P.O. Box 793, Lenox, MA 01240. 1–800–741–7353. Robin's spiritual home, this wonderful place provides a warm, unpressured, nondogmatic environment for retreats of all kinds. With many yoga classes every day to choose from, outstanding psychological, spiritual, and health-oriented programs, DansKinetics (yoga and dance), bodywork, and great food, in a gorgeous mountain setting, it is a truly special place for transformation and rest. Kripalu offers many women-oriented programs.

Omega Institute. 260 Lake Drive, Rhinebeck, NY 12752–3212. 1–800–944–1001. Offering programs on just about any new age topic you could imagine, Omega is a smorgasbord of spiritual delights. Lots of women-oriented programs on dance, art, writing, health, self-defense, yoga, singing, and on and on. A beautiful site and quality instructors. We spent a memorable week at one of their programs at Ghost Ranch in Abiquiu, New Mexico, on a women's wilderness retreat led by Colleen Kelley and Nancy Goddard.

Heart of the Goddess: Wholistic Center and Gallery. 10 Leopard Road, Berwyn, PA 19312. 610–695–9494. Hemitra Crecraft and Sue King started this women's center years ago as a manifestation of their own passions. Now they have a very nice gift shop and a ritual center. We attended a wonderful winter solstice program there, complete with Christmas carols with female-honoring lyrics. It was down to earth, mystical and a joy. HOTG offers many training programs and workshops, including Health Mastery Training, Woman Wisdom, and Reiki.

Tassajara Zen Mountain Monastery. Tassajara Reservations Office, 300 Page Street, San Francisco, CA 94102. 415–863–3136. This is a quiet place at the end of the road where you can take a deep breath and let go. It also happens to be a Zen monastery and hot springs spa. Guests are welcome from May through Labor Day weekend. Nestled in the lap of Gaia, in the wild Los Padres National Forest near Big Sur, California, accommodations are elegant/spartan, and the vegetarian food is famously celebrated. There are workshops and programs throughout the summer.

*Robin Deen Carnes (right), a former corporate human resources manager,
teaches YogaRhythmics^{SM}, a spiritually based blend of yoga and dance.*

*Sally Craig (left) is an organizational consultant, gardener, and drummer.
Together, they lead workshops on creating women's circles.*